School-I
and Their Prospects

KENNETH ROBERTS

School-Leavers and Their Prospects

Youth in the Labour Market in the 1980s

Open University Press

Milton Keynes

Open University Press
A division of
Open University Educational Enterprises Limited
12 Cofferidge Close, Stony Stratford, Milton Keynes MK11 1BY, England

First published 1984

British Library Cataloguing in Publication Data

Roberts, Kenneth, *1940-*
    School leavers and their prospects.
    1. High school graduates——Employment——
    Great Britain
    I. Title
    331.3′4′0941   HD6276.G7

ISBN-0-335-10418-5

Text design by W.A.P.

Typeset by Butler & Tanner Ltd, Frome, Somerset

Printed in Great Britain
by St Edmundsbury Press,
Bury St Edmunds, Suffolk

Contents

Preface   vii

1 Introduction   1
Before World War II   What's new?   Defining the problem

2 Education: a good start in life?   11
A sound investment?   School education   Further and higher education
The failure of reform   Standards   Technological illiterates   Careers
education   Credentialism

3 Post-war youth in the labour market   25
Training and further education for all?   Non-apprenticed youth   Industrial
training   Strain and turmoil?   Anticipatory socialization   Occupational
socialization   The decay of clear roads

4 Mass unemployment returns   45
The spread of joblessness   Why have young people's jobs disappeared?
Local labour markets   Qualifications   Contacts   Ethnic
minorities   Gender   Cyclical and structural problem?

5 What youth unemployment means   61
Rates and realities   What snapshots conceal   Public issues, personal
solutions   Sub-employment   Long-term youth unemployment   The
experience of unemployment   Is youth unemployment especially
damaging?   The social context

6 Government responses   78
Special measures   Job Creation Projects   The Youth Opportunities
Programme   The training for skills programme   Community
Industry   Verdicts on the Youth Opportunities Programme   The Young
Workers Scheme   Job splitting   The Youth Training Scheme   The right
approach?

7 **Alternatives**   98
Leisure   Training   Education   Jobs   Risks and opportunities

Bibliography   116

Index   129

Preface

This book analyses present-day school-leavers' predicaments. It examines the implications of long- and short-term economic trends, what successive governments have done, and what they have not, but might do to assist young people. The evidence is from my own and the many other recent studies of school-leavers entering the labour market, threatened by unemployment, better served than ever by schemes and courses, but less likely than at any time since World War II to find real jobs. However, the book is also derived from a longer period of research and debate on the transition from school to work. Until recently most of the debates were academic insofar as the wider society saw little cause to regard youth employment as a problem. The following chapters keep academics' professional problems in their proper place, in the background. The focus throughout is on present-day school-leavers' prospects. But earlier enquiries, which explained how transitions into the workforce were accomplished during the post-war full-employment decades, supply a useful benchmark from which to assess exactly how school-leavers' problems and opportunities have changed.

Readers whose interest in youth employment precedes the resurgence of mass youth unemployment may recognize that the following analysis builds directly upon my earlier work, which stressed the importance of opportunity structures as determinants of school-leavers' trajectories. This book explains how changes in and, in some cases, the collapse of, these structures—rather than school-leavers' own shortcomings—have been responsible for beginning workers' current difficulties, whose resolution, it is argued, will require a systematic reconstruction of their opportunities.

Some recent investigators have been startled by the resourcefulness of the young people at greatest risk, in devising their own solutions and coping with levels of unemployment that virtually all commentators condemn as intolerable. When jobs were plentiful, school-leavers impressed an earlier generation of researchers with their ability to reconcile themselves to—and, in many instances, their eagerness to enter—unskilled, careerless, low-paid jobs. School-leavers' expectations and aspirations have always reflected their opportunities, however depressing to detached observers. This book acknowledges the young unemployed's coping powers, just as earlier cohorts' ability to accept limited career prospects had to be recognized, but without condoning the necessity. Young people will prove equally capable of responding to educational, training and job opportunities that better serve their own and the wider society's long-term interests.

The following passages endeavour to clarify contemporary school-leavers' problems. The evidence and arguments may change some minds, but they will definitely not be the last word. They are offered as an interim contribution to a debate that is likely to continue into the 1990s. Youth in the labour market is now a social problem, arguably one of Britain's main domestic problems, rather than a topic of mere academic interest.

While accepting full and sole responsibility for the entire contents, I would like to express my appreciation and indebtedness to the stimulus of the many colleagues I have worked with and among, discussing and debating youth in the labour market over the last 20 years. In addition, my thanks are due to Susan Alexis Roberts who assisted in drafting, and Patricia McMillan who typed the manuscript.

K Roberts
Department of Sociology, University of Liverpool, 1983

1

Introduction

The return of mass youth unemployment has been accompanied by many diagnoses. Some blame young people themselves insofar as their attitudes, skills and qualifications are judged deficient by the standards set in modern industries. The second step in this argument is to criticize schools for failing to offer adequate vocational preparation. It says more about the distribution of ideological power than the real sources of young people's difficulties that unemployment has led to education- and school-leavers being questioned more strenuously than the economy. When there are insufficient jobs, someone must be at the back of the queue, unemployed, whatever the quality of the workforce. One reason for another book on youth in the labour market is to challenge the existing terms of debate, as well as to evaluate measures already implemented and under discussion.

Before World War II

The generations who grew to maturity in the 1950s and 1960s learnt from their own experience to take smooth transitions into the labour force for granted. They may regard the difficulties of school-leavers in the 1980s as a temporary dislocation. In fact, the transition into employment has been a problem throughout the greater part of industrial history. The smooth transitions of post-war decades were exceptions to the general rule. Recent school-leavers' difficulties are not unprecedented.

Young people have always been peripheral workers, sought in periods of labour shortages and denied jobs during recessions. They have always been cheap and therefore useful to marginal businesses. Beginning workers have been expected to perform tasks and accept conditions of employment that adults reject. Market economies inevitably generate marginal firms and jobs. They need peripheral workers, a sub-proletariat, whether they be women, immigrants or young people.

Child labour was an emotive nineteenth-century issue. The working child pre-dated industrialism, but the decay of the guilds that regulated apprenticeship in the Middle Ages, the removal of children from homes and families and their concentration in austere factories stirred Victorian reformers. Children were exposed to the full rigours of early capitalism: employed for long hours, from tender ages, for pitiful wages in factories, coal mines and sweeping chimneys. Reformers who sought to protect children from physical and moral damage had to struggle against *laissez-faire* doctrines and employers' perceived interests. Hence the fight was won only gradually and piecemeal, initially through Factory Acts covering specific industries which prohibited or restricted the employment of children below given ages, and sometimes insisted upon part-time education. Until World War I, the exploitation of children in sweated domestic and retail trades remained a live issue. It was only the enforcement of universal elementary schooling that finally relegated the child labour problem to history.

The 1918 Education Act removed the under-14s from the labour market, but youth employment remained a social problem. Unemployment was widespread, and many jobs offered to school-leavers led into blind alleys: the young people were dismissed when they grew too old and demanded or became eligible for adult rates. In the inter-war period a series of investigators sought to establish the real extent of youth unemployment. Official statistics were mistrusted. Many out-of-work youth failed to register because they were ineligible for 'the dole'. Eagar and Secretan (1925) traced ninety-four boys who left a Bermondsey school in 1923 and discovered that 'only' 25 per cent were unemployed at the time, although this was double the registered figure and nearly every boy had experienced unemployment since leaving school. Jewkes and Jewkes (1938) contacted 2,038 recent school-leavers in five Lancashire towns and found that, in the different areas, 17–36 per cent had been unemployed at some time. The Carnegie Trust sponsored an investigation among 18–25 year old males in Cardiff, Liverpool and Glasgow in the summer of 1937, and revealed unemployment rates of 20–30 per cent (Cameron, Lush and Meara, 1943). Many pre- and post-war studies of school-leavers concentrated on boys. Girls' unemployment, lack of training and further education were considered less of a problem.

The prevailing levels of unemployment throughout the inter-war years made the mis-employment of young people appear intractable. With so many seeking jobs, employers were able to use juveniles as a constant stream of cheap expendable labour. School-leavers were hired as errand boys, floor sweepers, messengers and suchlike, paid juvenile wages, and dismissed once they ceased to be juveniles. Apprentices sometimes suffered this treatment, finding their skills surplus to requirements once their time was served. Two-thirds of the jobs held by Eagar and Secretan's boys were blind alleys, temporary or casual. The Social Survey of Merseyside found that 74 per cent of the first jobs obtained by schoolleavers led to dead ends (Jones, 1934).

The problems facing school-leavers in the 1980s, the twin threats of unemployment and trash jobs, are not unprecedented, and the predictors of success among inter-war school-leavers still discriminate among young people in education, then in the labour market. 'Robust build' is the sole variable to have disappeared from research reports. Lewis (1924) followed up school-leavers from 450 unskilled households in Glasgow, Middlesborough and Blaenau Festiniog during 1919–21, and judged 30 per cent to be in poor health due to inadequate housing, clothing and nutrition. Healthy, well-developed school-leavers stood a better chance of winning employers' favour. A good school record and report were additional advantages. So was a father in regular work, particularly if he enjoyed good standing with foremen and works managers. Being 'spoken for' was, and remains, a normal means of obtaining sought-after employment. Family size and birth-order affected school-leavers' prospects. Older children from large families were required to earn as much as they could as soon as possible and were unlikely to be ushered into apprenticeships. Younger children, especially those with few siblings, were more fortunate. The inter-war investigations also noted the importance of family background as a source of 'temperament'. The bright, keen, punctual and reliable young people who impressed employers tended to have parents with 'progressive' outlooks who offered advice and encouragement. Pessimistic, cynical and apathetic parents seemed to rear young people with correspondingly poor temperaments, and so the cycle of deprivation continued (Bevington, 1933).

The inter-war enquiries that made the sharpest impression in their time were undoubtedly those that explored how young people's lives were scarred by unemployment. This was the principal concern of the Carnegie enquiry, which found that any holiday atmosphere was shortlived. It explained how young men without work soon became uneasy and lost confidence in their abilities, and how—as weeks and months wore on—many became unable to face the fruitless round of job seeking. Other investigators confirmed the young unemployed's loss of esteem and self-respect (Eagar and Secretan, 1925). They resented burdening their families. Loss of self-respect coupled with shortage of cash and, in time, their inability to dress respectably, gradually separated the unemployed from more fortunate acquaintances. The Carnegie researchers found that individuals from neighbourhoods where unemployment was exceptional were the most severely afflicted by guilt. Where joblessness was common, it was easier for individuals to accept the predicament. Instead of feeling guilty, many became indifferent, cynical and gradually abandoned standards as it became 'necessary', for example, to fiddle assistance claims and resort to crime. Investigators spoke of the young unemployed's personalities deteriorating with the loss of regular habits, when there was no need to get up at any particular time, dress well and practise work discipline. Eagar and Secretan expressed misgivings about young people learning the art of living without work, losing ambition, gravitating towards gambling and crime, and developing 'bolshevik attitudes'.

Not all pre-war school-leavers faced dole queues and blind alleys. Some obtained genuine apprenticeships and progressed to skilled, relatively secure jobs. Individuals from middle-class homes normally attended secondary schools, then obtained white-collar employment. Before World War I a scholarship ladder had been created enabling some bright working-class children to climb from elementary to secondary education and even into the universities. But few among the 80 per cent of the nation's children who left school aged 14 were sufficiently secure to be untroubled by the prospects of unemployment and dead-end jobs.

What's new?

Contemporary school-leavers' difficulties are not unprecedented but neither are they identical to the problems of the 1930s. Youth unemployment in the 1980s is partly concealing, while simultaneously interacting with and aggravating, additional trends that have no exact historical parallels.

Firstly, the social selection that once occurred in primary schools then at age 11 has been deferred. The principal educational issue of the last thirty years, the 11-plus, is now resolved. The battle for comprehensives has been won. These schools are here to stay, to educate the majority of young people. There are few votes in reviving secondary moderns. Grammar schools retain supporters but there are no examples of parents campaigning for their children's right to a secondary modern education. However, as the 11-plus recedes into history it is becoming clear that the discontents that led to its demise have not disappeared but been displaced. Once-and-for-all selection at 11 has been replaced by selection within comprehensives, often at 14-plus into 'O'-level, CSE and non-examination streams—a process that arouses all the familiar anxieties and causes as many heartbreaks.

There is an even more decisive selection at the age of 16. Some young people proceed from compulsory schooling to further education and training which leads to secure and progressive careers. Others are left on the margins of the workforce, either unemployed or in jobs, schemes and courses with no guaranteed prospects. Like the secondary modern, these 'youth opportunities' are often waiting rooms where young people mark time. The wider society's solutions to their unemployment have now joined many school-leavers' problems.

Unemployment exacerbates the 16-plus problem. The gap between the winners and losers is all too visible. Yet if the jobs that awaited beginning workers in the 1960s could be returned, the school-leavers of the 1980s would be less impressed. Young people's life chances and aspirations are no longer tailored by streaming in primary schools followed by selection at 11 which prevented the majority even competing for credentials and entertaining hopes of success. Wider educational opportunities have unblocked young people's aspirations, while the consolation for failure—an early entry into well-paid if often monotonous and careerless jobs—has been withdrawn. Sixteen-year-old school-leavers now face training schemes, courses and jobs paying youth wages, and few of these opportunities offer clear roads to adult employment. There is no guarantee that all young people will emerge from their 'transitions', but there is a real danger that some will be scarred for life, embittered towards a society that is unable or unwilling to provide the jobs for which schooling prepared them.

The frustrations and controversies formerly associated with selection within compulsory education now surround the opportunities that follow. The futility of addressing social class, gender and racial inequalities in primary and secondary education, when these divisions resurface with a vengeance the moment young people enter the labour market, is already apparent. In the 1960s it was hoped that educational reforms would widen the life chances of inner-urban youth. The problem of the 1980s is that higher educational standards often lead to near-zero job prospects. Inadequate opportunities at 16-plus can demoralize secondary school-teachers and pupils. Many of the latter drop out, psychologically if not physically, long before their compulsory education is complete.

The changing shape of the occupational structure is a second development which alone and unaided, given time, would have undermined transitions into employment. The number of manufacturing jobs is declining and this trend will continue. If industrial jobs are replaced, most of their successors will be tertiary occupations, designing and maintaining technological systems, and providing financial, personal, health, recreational, educational and other services (Stonier, 1983).

There is scope for argument about the proportions of jobs likely to be upgraded and degraded by these trends. Another argument questions the value of assessing new occupations against conventional notions of skill. New jobs may require different types rather than more or less of the talents employed by traditional craftsmen. There is further debate on whether skilled status has ever rested primarily on the technical complexity of the work tasks. Claims to skilled status may have been conceded by bemused customers and clients, and sometimes by knowledgeable employers as a partly non-monetary reward in exchange for loyalty, co-operation and 'responsible' behaviour. These debates will be engaged, where relevant, in subsequent chapters. For present purposes it is sufficient to note that no-one believes that the school syllabuses, opportunities for further education and on-the-job training offered to young people in the 1960s and 1970s would have continued to satisfy the economy's labour requirements.

Britain's methods of vocational training proved less satisfactory than her main European competitors' in the post-war reconstruction and subsequent growth of industry. Nearly a half of young people left school at the earliest opportunity, lost contact with formal education for ever and were given no opportunity to acquire skills, on any definition. Britain's methods of equipping young people with vocational skills permitted survival but not success in the industrial era. If they had not been destroyed by recession and unemployment, these opportunities would have equipped neither young people nor the wider society for a post-industrial future.

A third change is that adulthood has become less certain, more fluid. Adolescence used to be a transitional phase between two known statuses—childhood and adulthood. Children's roles were clearly defined by their homes and schools. By the time they were emancipated from childhood, the adult roles that awaited individuals were known and visible. The problems of youth were essentially transitional. School-leavers needed 'bridges' which would provide them with the additional skills, and technical and social qualifications that were needed to tackle adult jobs. Similarly, adolescents needed to disengage from their families of orientation, select partners, then establish themselves as husbands and wives in families of procreation.

This view of youth as a transitional phase between known and secure statuses is fast becoming obsolete. Social selection is no longer completed before the end of compulsory schooling. In addition, the pace of technical and occupational change is undermining traditional, life-long occupational careers based on qualifications and skills acquired prior to entering adult jobs. Changes of occupation during adulthood are becoming the norm, not the exception. Traditional gender roles are being challenged. Family life is also changing. Life-long monogamy is now just one of several patterns. The trends are towards a succession of sexual and marital partners. Rather than basing life styles upon stable occupational and domestic statuses, many individuals now appear to spend their entire lives in transition.

Successful entry into the world of work used to involve becoming attached to specific skills, occupations and organizations. 'Maturity' used to mean intimate dependence on one opposite-sexed partner. Maintaining or repairing the bridges that supported traditional transitions will not prepare today's youth for their futures. They must learn flexibility and adaptability, to disengage as well as to attach themselves to occupations, sexual and domestic companions.

Defining the problem

Chapters 2 and 3 review the recent past. They explain how transitions into employment were accomplished in the 1950s and 1960s when jobs awaited virtually all school-leavers in most parts of the country. The purpose is not to sketch a model for restoration. Solutions to current school-leavers' problems must confront the new realities of the 1980s. However, every generation rewrites history to satisfy its own preoccupations, and the spread of unemployment has already inspired reappraisals of post-war educational trends. Some claim that the abandonment of streaming and early selection, the spread of child-centred progressive methods and the emphasis on passing examinations rather than acquiring practical skills have helped to make the 1980s' school-leavers unemployable. It is argued that young people would be better placed to compete for jobs if schools went back to basics and ensured that all children became accomplished in reading, writing and arithmetic, and if teachers disciplined pupils into habitual obedience then added practical skills and knowledge. Chapter 2 exposes the flaws in these arguments. Elementary schooling did not save the school-leavers of the 1930s from unemployment. Comprehensive schools and progressive teaching did not prevent post-war school-leavers making smooth transitions when jobs were available. Aspects of education that industrialists criticize have often arisen in response to employers' behaviour. For instance, industry has reserved its most attractive careers for young people with academic credentials not technical skills.

Some commentators have recently added insult to injury by suggesting that the replacement of school-leavers' jobs with schemes and courses amounts to progress. They argue that abrupt transitions into the entirely different world of work for which they were ill-prepared proved traumatic for young school-leavers. The new technical courses, work experience and training schemes are approved for enabling young people to make gradual transitions, taking stock of their abilities and interests before making irrevocable career decisions. Chapter 3 explains that the vast majority of school-leavers in the 1950s and 1960s coped with abrupt transitions with little difficulty. Their main problem was not the transition itself but the quality of some awaiting jobs, for industry never implemented its full share of the promised post-war reforms.

Gradual transitions can be over-rated. Part-time employment prior to school-leaving is associated with educational failure not occupational success. Part-time further education on day release and evening classes is notorious for high failure and drop-out rates. In contrast, sandwich courses in higher education appear to satisfy students and employers. The success of phased transitions depends upon the types of education and employment that are involved, and the proportions in which they are mixed. However, abrupt transitions are within the coping powers of most school-leavers and university graduates. Whether young workers settle has always depended primarily on the quality of their jobs rather than the speed of their transfer from education.

Solutions to beginning workers' difficulties are bound to fail when based on mistaken definitions of the problems to be tackled. Chapters 4 and 5 explain exactly how and why youth unemployment has spread since the mid-1970s. They describe how the employment side of young people's former bridges collapsed, undermined by economic recession, how different groups of school-leavers have been affected and how they react.

Chapter 6 outlines governments' responses; the Job Creation Projects, the Work Experience Programme, the Youth Opportunities Programme (YOP) followed by the Youth Training Scheme (YTS). There is a huge credibility gap between official accounts and young people's experiences of these measures. Scheme organizers and course tutors often find themselves at the centre of this conflict. Not even the providers consider existing measures a total solution to beginning workers' difficulties. Even if they eradicate youth unemployment, which seems unlikely, they will not equip beginning workers with the skills new occupations require. Nor will they resolve the discontents surrounding selection at 16-plus. It is painfully obvious that special measures have been devised for other people's children. Programme directors and consenting politicians are not seeking these opportunities for their own offspring. In time, the intended beneficiaries (or victims) will reject second-best treatment following compulsory education, just as an earlier generation became dissatisfied with the secondary moderns.

Chapter 7 appraises alternative policies that could supplement or replace existing measures. It makes the case for extending rather than rolling back the post-war educational reforms, and for real training and jobs initiatives. It also examines the political implications of the alternative ways in which the entry into employment might be restructured, and why vested interests feel threatened.

While attributing school-leavers' difficulties mainly to economic failure and insisting that the employment side of their routes into working life must be rebuilt, this book is not a sustained call to overthrow the present economy. Youth unemployment is easily embraced by critiques of capitalism, but the assimilation is usually a cop-out, a way of avoiding instead of tackling school-leavers' problems. It is fair and reasonable to point out that risks of unemployment are inherent in market economies where employers sift would-be workers and use the threat of the dole to discipline labour to compete for jobs. Under *laissez-faire* capitalism, transition problems are borne mainly by young people. Private property biases market forces so that conflicts of interests appear naturally resolved in employers' favour. When there is insufficient demand for labour, school-leavers are left coping with unemployment. Market pressures do not oblige firms to support surplus workers.

The cop-out is to create an impression that there are reliable solutions to current school-leavers' problems whose application is impeded solely by capitalist interests. Existing socialist regimes in the USSR and Eastern Europe may appear to have resolved their young people's transition difficulties. They organize induction into employment as an aspect of educational and economic planning. Employers are obliged to respect young people's rights to employment, training and continuing education. These societies offer consumers less choice and restrict the political liberties that western nations prize, but they ease many burdens to which all workers—including newcomers to the labour force—are exposed in market economies. However, socialist planning cannot guarantee that all people receive relevant and effective on-the-job training and continuing education, or even that all those 'in employment' are usefully occupied.

What to do on Monday, the types of jobs, education and training to offer to different groups of young people, remains basically the same problem following the overthrow of capitalism, and it is not self-evident that young people's difficulties are incapable of solution without abolishing private property and economic markets. Many former transition problems were eased if not eradicated by the 'new deal' offered to young people after 1945 when education, training and job opportunities were enlarged. These solutions did not last. There can be no 'for-all-time' solutions to young people's problems in changing societies, capitalist or socialist. Only when we have decided what opportunities are needed to resolve late twentieth-century youth employment problems will it become possible to judge whether a socialist or a capitalist context will prove the more hospitable. The final chapter explains how both capitalism and socialism can support solutions to young people's difficulties. Each must be judged on the attractiveness of its solutions, rather than by claiming a unique capacity or alleging a complete inability to tackle young people's problems.

2

Education:
A Good Start in Life?

A sound investment?

No-one ever believed that more education would automatically mean better vocational preparation. Nevertheless, throughout the 1950s and 1960s there was widespread faith that all types of educational investment—whether in primary, secondary, further or higher education— would pay economic dividends in the long term. Economists encouraged this view of education as an investment in human capital—boosting the quality of the future workforce. This was the era when educators learnt to take growth for granted.

Few teachers have ever seen themselves, first and foremost, as servants of industry. Promoting economic growth was only one of many educational objectives. Others included personal development and equality of opportunity. Until the 1970s, however, debates were about priorities. In the long run there appeared no conflict between developing every child's talents to the full, releasing life chances from social origins and increasing the value of the economy's human capital. Researchers and industrialists who queried whether, measured against vocational requirements, the growth of educational spending was raising standards, made little impression upon policy makers until the Great Debate, led by Prime Minister Callaghan who suggested in 1977 that schools might have paid too much attention to social and personal gains, at the expense of young people's need to learn how to earn their livings (Department of Education and Science, 1977).

Subsequently educational policy has been about cut-backs, not growth. The educational developments of earlier decades have been accused of aggravating, if not causing, recent school-leavers' employment problems. Education's critics argue that if schools were vocationally effective, employers would be competing for newly qualified school-leavers, while other age-groups would be feeling the force of the recession. According to this argument, full employment temporarily concealed education's deficiencies, whereas in tighter labour markets— where employers possess scope for choice—young people have been left at the end of the queue. Chapter 4 will explain that since the mid-1970s unemployment has risen more rapidly and to higher levels among 16–18 year olds than in any other age-group. Have recent school-leavers been paying the price for education's misuse of the growth decades? This diagnosis appeals to those who spent the 1960s predicting that more would mean worse, deploring progressive methods and warning that comprehensives threatened standards. Has state education declined into such a mess that bright young people need rescuing via assisted places into independent schools, that a voucher system is required to expose all schools to market pressures, and that the task of piloting 'relevant' courses must be handed to the Manpower Services Commission (MSC)? Is the return of mass youth unemployment proof that the educational policies and trends of the 1950s and 1960s failed to equip young people to compete for jobs, and must be reversed? Early measures to alleviate youth unemployment embodied the view that young people were inadequately prepared for the labour market and needed 'work experience', even 'social and life skills' to render them employable.

As already indicated, and as the following chapters will explain in detail, my own view is that any accurate reading of recent history shows that current school-leavers' difficulties are products of economic failure, not post-war educational policies. Like other remedies based on a false diagnosis, attempts to achieve a closer integration between education and manpower requirements by pressuring schools to produce more employable 16 year olds will aggravate rather than resolve the latter's problems.

School education

The 1944 Education Act decreed secondary education for all, and envisaged three types of schools catering for children with different interests, aptitudes and abilities. Grammar, technical and modern schools were to educate academic, in-between and practical children. Each type of school was intended to provide a secondary education suited to its clientele. The schools were not to be better and worse, but simply different, and to ensure parity the 1944 Education Act provided for the school-leaving age to be raised to 16 so that basic courses in all secondary schools would be of equal length. Equality was delayed until 1973, but 15 became the minimum leaving age in 1947. In addition, after 1944 teachers in all schools were paid on the same salary scales—another measure intended to create parity.

Fee-paying in local authority schools was abolished. After 1944 only a limited number of direct grant schools were allowed to remain under independent management and admit fee-paying in addition to 'scholarship' pupils while receiving support from public funds. In 1944 there was talk of integrating the remaining independent schools (Fleming Report, 1944). This talk has subsequently ebbed and flowed. Fee-paying schools have continued to fill a disproportionate share of places at Oxbridge and in the most prestigious professions, and this situation has provoked periodic calls for their abolition or integration. The former would interfere with 'parental rights' while the latter would be expensive, so reformers' zeal has usually been deflected towards raising standards in state schools thereby erasing the advantages that ability to pay has conferred. In 1976 the Labour government began to phase-out direct grant schools, but before their final disappearance the 1979 Conservative administration introduced an assisted-places scheme.

Contrary to post-war hopes, the issue of private education has never been consensually resolved, but by the end of the 1940s over 90 per cent of children were educated in LEA primary schools, then faced the 11-plus and were subsequently allocated to different types of secondary schools according to their abilities, not parental means. This process of allocation never worked as intended. Parents stubbornly but correctly regarded the 11-plus as a pass–fail hurdle. It became a source of immense anxiety for pupils and parents who considered secondary modern education inferior, not just different. In retrospect, it is easy to appreciate that the prestige of the occupations to which they led was bound to affect parents' assessments of the different secondary schools. The concept of technical education never caught on. No-one ever identified a type of child with specifically technical abilities. The technical schools that existed in 1940s soon became imitations of the grammar schools, preparing pupils for GCE examinations (Edwards, 1960). In most parts of the country the 1944 Education Act led to bi-partite, not tri-partite secondary schooling.

During the 1950s dissatisfaction with the opportunities available in secondary moderns gelled into a powerful critique of the 11-plus. Researchers fuelled the discontent (Pedley, 1963). They drew attention to the victims of 11-plus selection—the borderline cases, the late developers, and children who failed to perform their true ability on the examination day. It was noted that children's chances of gaining grammar school places depended on their places of residence since LEAs allocated different proportions of children to the different types of schools (Douglas, 1964). In addition, researchers discovered that success and failure at age 11 were related to pupils' social class backgrounds and the 11-plus was indicted for its bias against working-class children (Benn and Simon, 1970). It was argued that an education system that labelled approximately 75 per cent of the nation's children as failures at age 11 was bound to waste talent, and would prove incapable of meeting an advanced industrial economy's need for highly educated and qualified manpower.

By 1959 the Labour Party had adopted the case for abolishing the 11-plus and educating all secondary-age children in comprehensives (Parkinson, 1970), and by 1980 the hurdle has ceased to exist in most parts of the country; 80 per cent of adolescents were attending comprehensive schools. This reorganization was accomplished without repealing or replacing the 1944 legislation. Supporters of comprehensives believed that these schools would fulfill not change the Act's aims. Removing the 11-plus barrier that impeded working-class children in particular was considered essential to allow all pupils to receive an education suited to their abilities, which had been the intention of the 1944 legislation.

The campaign against the 11-plus coincided with a movement to enlarge the numbers of secondary pupils entering public examinations, who would then hopefully leave school with recognized certificates of attainment. The GCE 'O'-levels were originally designed for the top 20 per cent, the academic children in grammar schools, but by the end of the 1950s they were being used more widely. Many secondary moderns had established examination streams, smaller numbers had sixth forms, and these schools were transforming themselves into comprehensives in all but name (Taylor, 1963). The schools found that they contained children with the necessary talent, and even pupils who found academic syllabuses extremely demanding had to be given the opportunity to take them—or so it seemed to many parents and teachers, for school-leavers' future careers could hinge on their paper qualifications.

All the committees that considered 'examinations' recognized that written tests were inappropriate for some children and subjects, especially the practical varieties, and that no examination could test all the qualities that schools aimed to foster (Crowther, 1959; Beloe, 1960; Newsom, 1963). Nevertheless it was argued that many pupils beneath the 'O'-level band and their teachers would benefit from the incentive of a public examination, and to meet these demands the Certificate of Secondary Education (CSE) was introduced in 1965.

Like so many educational reforms, the CSE has never worked as its architects originally intended. The exam was aimed at the remainder of the top half of the ability range for whom 'O'-levels were too demanding, but it was soon being used more extensively. By 1980 over a half of all pupils were being entered for at least one 'O'-level. Some sat mixtures of 'O'-level and CSE exams, often doubling up, taking CSEs as a precaution against failing 'O'-levels. The bottom half, not the second quartile of the ability range, was taking CSEs only and less than a fifth of all school-leavers possessed no qualifications whatsoever.

Few educators approve of the extent to which Britain's comprehensives have become exam factories. The case for merging 'O'-levels and CSEs into a common system of exams, thereby eradicating the practice of doubling-up and protecting pupils of moderate abilities who are currently entered for 'O'-levels with little chance of obtaining the passes considered essential before proceeding to 'A'-levels, has been generally accepted. However, the interested parties—governments, examining boards, universities and teachers' organizations—have found it difficult to agree on any set of reforms.

Many teachers consider written examinations inappropriate for children of limited academic talent for whom the secondary moderns were originally intended. 'Newsom children', as they became known following a government report on the secondary schooling of 'half our future' (Newsom, 1963), have been considered more likely to develop their abilities in classrooms and workshops free from examination pressures. Yet since the raising of the school-leaving age to 16 in 1973, the majority of these children have entered CSEs. Schools have found it impossible to resist the scramble for credentials. The young people need certificates to strengthen their claims in the job market. Employers are less impressed by school reports and character references, and parents insist that their children be given the opportunity to win recognized qualifications.

Supporters of comprehensives have been united only in their opposition to the 11-plus. There has never been any agreement on how a comprehensive school should be organized (Bellaby 1977). Is a school truly comprehensive if it simply gathers grammar and secondary modern streams under one roof? Or does comprehensive mean merging pupils in mixed-ability groups? Few comprehensives avoid some form of ability grouping. Exam preparation usually requires pupils to be divided to study different 'O'-level and CSE syllabuses. Some enthusiasts hoped that comprehensive schools would offer all pupils a comprehensive education—a mixture of the academic, technical and practical subjects that were once intended for different children. However, if there has been any mixing of these syllabuses, grammar school education has proved the strongest ingredient. The academic education of the brightest children has not been diluted (Stevens, 1980), and in so far as the schooling of all secondary pupils has become exam-oriented, it can be argued that the less able are now being exposed to 'watered down' versions of the grammar school tradition.

Many less able children, and some of the brightest, become frustrated and disillusioned during the examination rat race. In London, on a typical school-day, 25 per cent of fifth-year pupils are absent. There are additional respects in which comprehensives have disappointed their supporters. Inequalities in the attainments of children from different social class and ethnic backgrounds (Ford, 1969), and the channelling of girls and boys into feminine and masculine subjects, have survived comprehensive re-organization.

Education has never lacked reformers, but until the return of youth unemployment the majority planned to build upon, not dismantle, the progress of the post-war decades. The 1944 Education Act and subsequent comprehensives re-organization appeared to be fulfilling some of their aims. The bi-partite system was considered an advance on the former situation where, unless they were bright enough to win scholarships and sometimes even then, children's chances of receiving secondary schooling depended on their parents' ability to pay. Some comprehensives may have achieved little more than gathering grammar school and other children under one roof, but even so, it could be argued that the schools catered for late-developers and avoided the sometimes arbitrary and irreversible treatment of borderline cases. The numbers of pupils entering public examinations rose throughout the 1950s, 1960s and 1970s. Since 1970 there has been no increase in the proportion obtaining at least five 'O'-levels and subsequently the three 'A'-levels usually demanded for university entry, but the numbers passing some 'O'-levels (and often CSEs as well) have grown, as have the 'new sixth-formers' taking one or two 'A'-levels and maybe repeating 'O'-levels rather than preparing for higher education. Whatever problems remained, until the mid-1970s few educationalists doubted that the trends were in the right direction—towards raising standards and widening opportunities.

Further and higher education

Recently more young people have been remaining longer in school then leaving with qualifications, and one sequel has been an expansion of further and higher education. Further education was a major growth sector in the 1950s. The numbers of young workers benefiting from day release and attending evening classes, taking courses ranging from City and Guilds to Higher National Certificates, increased steadily. In 1956 selected institutions were designated as Colleges of Advanced Technology (CATs) and a new qualification, the Diploma in Technology (Dip Tech) was introduced to accommodate the growing band on advanced courses, and to give further impetus to high-level studies in technology and applied science. Since 1956 maintenance grants for all students on degree-level course, not just in universities, have been mandatory. However, opportunities in higher education did not expand as rapidly as the numbers leaving school with entry qualifications. Competition for places became increasingly fierce, and with 'the bulge', the products of the post-war baby boom passing through the secondary schools, the Robbins Committee was appointed to consider the future of higher education (Robbins, 1963).

This committee predicted (accurately) that the numbers of qualified applicants would continue to grow and, indeed, would double within a decade, and enunciated its famous principle that higher education should be available for all who were qualified and wished to proceed. This main recommendation was accepted by the government of the day. The outcome was an expansion of the old, and the creation of the new, 'plate glass' universities. In addition to recommending expansion the Committee criticized the distinction between university students who earned degrees and those pursuing degree-level studies often of greater vocational relevance in other institutions including CATs, who were awarded different, less prestigeous qualifications. Most former CATs, thereafter, were transformed into technological universities, BEd courses for trainee teachers were introduced in Colleges of Education, and the Council for National Academic Awards (CNAA) was created to validate courses and award degrees to the remaining students pursuing advanced studies outside universities.

It appeared that university education was to be Britain's predominant type of higher education until 1966 when the government announced a binary policy and designed new Polytechnics—institutions within the LEA sector that were to concentrate on advanced courses, particularly in applied science and technology. Why was an alternative to universities considered necessary? The universities were reluctant to cater for certain aspiring students, including those wishing to study part-time and/or without orthodox entry qualifications—'O'-levels and 'A'-levels (Robinson, 1968). Moreover, since Polytechnics are situated within the LEA sector, it is easier for governments to influence their academic priorities and discourage, for example, any swing towards the arts and humanities. Governments have also suspected, though the case is still unproven, that higher education can be offered in less expensive surroundings than British universities.

The Colleges of Education expanded during the 1960s, adding to the opportunities in higher education. Following 'the bulge' the birth rate did not stabilize close to its pre-war level, but rose from 1955 to 1965 creating pressure on school places and teacher shortages in primary then secondary education. Within secondary schools, demand for teachers was also boosted by 'the trend', as it became known, towards voluntary staying-on, then in 1973 by raising the school-leaving-age to 16.

During the 1970s the growth era ended. A declining birth rate from 1965 to 1977 led to falling rolls in primary then secondary schools, and cut-backs in teacher training. Some colleges closed. Others transformed themselves into Colleges of *Higher* Education and diversified their teaching, offering BA and BSc courses in addition to their BEd programmes. Growth in the universities and polytechnics only kept pace with the increasing numbers of school-leavers, and result of the rising birth rate eighteen years earlier. Since the early 1970s, the proportion of school-leavers proceeding to higher education, approximately 13 per cent, has been stable. In the early 1980s this proportion actually declined when the government ordered a slight reduction in student numbers. Since 1970 the Open University has been a rare growth point in British higher education, but this institution caters for adults, not school-leavers.

The failure of reform

The 1960s was a decade of reform and disillusion. The welfare state was accused of perpetuating, not alleviating poverty. Homelessness was identified as a growing problem despite massive post-war public housing programmes that had left local authorities owning a third of the nation's dwellings. This was the setting in which educational researchers demonstrated that despite the 1944 Education Act, the spread of comprehensives and the expansion of higher education, social origins remained as divisive as ever. It was difficult to discern even a trend towards equality of opportunity. College students, the principal beneficiaries of post-war educational expansion, reflected the disenchantment. They began to protest instead of expressing gratitude, and joined the counter-culture instead of nestling into the system.

One response urged more reform. Community education was proposed to engage the many pupils who found orthodox subjects boring, and experienced their latter years at school as a period of detention. Positive discrimination was favoured to nurture working-class pupils' talents through Educational Priority Areas in Britain, and in Operation Headstart, Wider Horizons and other US compensatory programmes that were launched as strides towards President Johnson's Great Society. Optimists are still convinced that with further reform and investment education will change society (Halsey, Heath and Ridge, 1980). But by the early 1970s contrary voices were audible. Deschoolers claimed that schools were ineffective educators, that their main functions were child custody, indoctrination and social selection, and that the cause of education would be best served by deschooling society (Illich, 1971; Reimer, 1971). Attacks on particular types of schools and teaching had been commonplace, but this tirade against schooling itself was novel. In Britain the case for deschooling never won a serious political hearing, but it helped to undermine the earlier confidence that equated post-war expansion with progress.

Between 1969 and 1975 a series of five *Black Papers* by right-wing intellectuals and politicians helped to inspire a 'back to basics' movement (Cox and Dyson, 1969 etc). They criticized post-war educational trends towards child-centred progressive methods and mixed-ability classes, and favoured a return to streaming, traditional teaching, defence of the remaining grammar schools, and maintaining standards in higher education. This onslaught encountered fierce opposition but succeeded in defining the ground for debate (Centre for Contemporary Cultural Studies, 1981) By the time youth unemployment became a national problem, education was on the defensive, and the misgivings of radicals and conservatives have become fused in a series of charges which accuse the schools of failing to equip people to compete for jobs.

Standards

Firstly, schools are accused of failing to maintain or, at least, not raising standards alongside the expansion of educational budgets and young people's school careers. Teachers can point out that in terms of examination successes standards have risen. Judged by its own yardsticks, education is a huge success, but critics allege that schools have been erecting their own while neglecting the standards set by the occupations for which young people must eventually compete.

In addition to deploring their competence in elementary school skills, employers have become critical of young people's attitudes and motivation. Teachers no longer rule by fear. Progressive schools operate by winning pupils' consent. Good teachers capture pupils' imaginations and encourage self-discipline. But what happens when pupils are uninterested in education and/or exposed to ineffective teachers? Employers complain that many of these school-leavers are virtually unemployable; that they are unwilling to follow rules, respect authority or perform routine operations diligently. The young people are accused of lax time-keeping and other irresponsible acts. Is schooling which allows young people to 'do their own thing' a suitable preparation for earning a living? In the years of full employment, firms had no option but to bear the costs of hiring school-leavers. Recession has widened employers' scope for choice and, it is argued, has exposed beginning workers' inadequacies.

These charges are easily rebutted. To begin with, school-leavers' performances on tests of reading and arithmetic have not declined. There has been a slight improvement since the 1950s. Some employers who complain might be better occupied inspecting their own standards. Many firms sift applicants using interviews and out-of-date tests interpreted by untrained personnel. Tests of vocational abilities often prove completely unrelated to the skills required in the jobs.

Young people have become more ambitious. Their aspirations are no longer conditioned by early selection. Employers are probably correct in their view that young people have become less willing to settle as malleable and obedient subordinates. However, the next chapter will explain why, instead of criticizing the schools, firms would be better employed creating training and career opportunities to satisfy young people's aspirations and the economy's future skill requirements.

Technological illiterates

Secondly, schools are accused of neglecting technical education. The facts on which these criticisms are based are not in dispute. During the growth decades technical schools and courses all but disappeared. Comprehensives offer pupils either full-strength or diluted versions of the former grammar school, academic curriculum. Many young people survive eleven years of compulsory education without being introduced to useful workshop, laboratory and office skills. Computers are now installed in most factories and offices, but some school-leavers are still unable to use keyboards.

Short episodes of 'work experience' have been introduced and by 1977 were offered in a third of all secondary schools (Carmichael, 1976; Institute of Careers Officers, 1977), but only 7 per cent of pupils were benefiting. The overwhelming majority of these judged the experience helpful, but schools have been reluctant to allow this innovation to interfere with pupils' academic progress.

Researchers have confirmed the wide gap between school syllabuses and business acumen (Moor, 1976). Over a half of the brighter pupils who proceed to 'A'-levels are allowed to drop maths and science at 16 if not before. Applied science, engineering and technology are accorded low status in education. These subjects are considered suitable only for less able students. Technological universities, even polytechnics, have endeavoured to raise their status through 'academic drift', by introducing pure science, social science and arts courses, thereby subverting the aim of enhancing the prestige of vocational education (Burgess and Pratt, 1974). Proposals to ensure that all young people develop basic numeracy and scientific intelligence, and to discourage the 'brightest and best' from becoming technological illiterates have a long history. In 1980 the Central Policy Review Staff (the government's 'think-tank') proposed a compulsory core curriculum and higher pay to attract well-qualified and capable maths and science teachers. Action is still awaited.

The flaw in using this evidence to condemn education lies in overlooking the fact that technical jobs are accorded low status in British industry. Schools and universities are willing to teach useful skills and knowledge when students' and teachers' efforts are rewarded, as in schools of medicine, dentistry, law and architecture. In neglecting technical courses and practical skills, education has only been mirroring industry's values. If firms wish to persuade more teachers and pupils to concentrate on applied science and technology, the means lie in their own hands. They must raise the salaries and widen the career opportunities of young people who pursue these courses.

Careers education

A third charge against education is that its efforts to provide careers information and advice are paltry and ineffective. These criticisms have been made repeatedly since the 1950s (Carter, 1966; Allen and Smith 1975; West and Newton, 1983), but careers remains a Cinderella of the curriculum (Department of Education and Science, 1979). Thomas and Wetherall's (1974) national enquiry discovered no school with a full-time careers teacher, and only 40 per cent of pupils had 'careers' as a regularly timetabled subject.

Neglect of 'careers' occurs at all levels in the academic hierarchy. When invited to look back upon their final year at school, recent leavers in all parts of Britain have complained of the failure of education to equip them for the labour market (Keil, 1978; Youthaid, 1979; Pollock and Nicholson, 1981; West and Newton, 1983). University undergraduates complain about their lack of careers and even educational guidance (Ching, 1970). Kaneti-Barry *et al*'s survey of over 2000 sixth formers (1971) found that only 18 per cent had discussed further education courses with teachers. Most students enter college without definite career intentions. British universities retain an ivory tower charm which has survived persistent external criticism and government exhortation to tailor courses to job requirements. The universities provide few occupational role models for students to emulate or evaluate, and do not encourage vocational exploration. Even vocational courses presume prior commitment (Kelsall *et al*., 1972; Gothard, 1982).

Careers advisers have a vested interest in developing their occupation, but would school-leavers benefit from more vocational guidance? The next chapter will explain that their lack of information and uncertain ambitions did not prevent young people settling in employment when jobs were awaiting. Furthermore, there is no evidence in Britain or any other country of careers education enhancing subsequent job satisfaction or career success (Roberts, 1977). Whatever efforts schools make, vocational preparation will always be incomplete prior to young people entering the labour market and gaining first-hand experience in real jobs. Newcomers to the workforce will always be ill-informed, unsure of their objectives and lacking in technical skills. Only industry itself can rectify these deficiencies. At the point of entering the workforce, vagueness and uncertainty can prove useful by increasing young people's willingness to accept the jobs they find available. Would a changing economy be able to accommodate recruits who were fully informed about all occupations, who knew exactly which jobs they wanted, and who were not prepared to compromise?

'Careers' may still be a Cinderella in the official curriculum, but a 'hidden curriculum' has always offered excellent vocational preparation. The types of secondary schools and, within comprehensives, the streams into which pupils are tracked have enabled them to assess their prospects and encouraged realistic, usually modest aspirations (Roberts, 1968a, 1968b, 1975, 1981a; Ashton and Field, 1976; Willis, 1977). Whatever other charges stick, education cannot be accused of impairing school-leavers' willingness to work. All investigators have found the majority of young people eagerly awaiting their 'release'. In some cases the boredom and aimlessness of school appear to increase teenagers' enthusiasm to leave and enter employment. School-leavers' attitudes towards work, knowledge of occupations and aspirations cannot be blamed for their current difficulties in establishing themselves in the workforce.

Credentialism

Freeman (1971) claims that in the USA 'the trend towards an increasingly professional, college-trained workforce will produce a more classical labour market'. Occuptional requirements, it is argued, are reflected in starting salaries. In turn, the argument runs, course enrolments are sensitive to salary prospects, and the college system is sufficiently flexible to adapt to changes in student demand. These are the mechanisms through which human capital theorists claim that education is regulated to produce young people with the qualifications and skills that employers seek.

During the last decade a rival theory has appeared alleging that education confers qualifications which grant access, but which are no proof of competence to perform well-rewarded jobs (Squires, 1979). According to Berg (1973), education is a 'great training robbery' which deceives and, in the long run, injures students and employers. There is impressive evidence that qualified recruits prove no more competent than other entrants in many occupations for which educational credentials have become essential passports. What makes the robbery possible? Collins (1979) argues that educational qualifications have become a 'cultural currency'. Occupations raise their status by demanding as high an entry price as possible. Students earn career opportunities by acquiring credentials. The net result is a qualification spiral in which students' appetite for credentials reduces their market value, which fuels demand for qualifications to still higher levels.

Economic ailments have been traced to this 'bureaupathology' or 'diploma disease' (Berg, 1973; Dore, 1976). Educationally successful young people are encouraged to consider themselves entitled to lifetimes of privilege before they have proved, and—in some cases—despite their proven lack of vocational competence. Educational failures become frustrated, bored and abandon ambition prior to testing their vocational abilities. Business organizations staff key positions with complacent incompetents, while potentially capable employees are prevented from using or even discovering their true abilities. It is argued that the quality of education also suffers. Schooling becomes exam cramming, while the joys of learning for its own sake and acquiring useful skills are lost (Dore, 1976).

Education stands accused of inflaming the diploma disease. Throughout the 1950s and 1960s schools and colleges were absorbing more and more resources to encourage more and more young people to join the rat race without, it is alleged, attempting to gear courses to job requirements. However, these accusations conveniently overlook the fact that it is industry's willingness to recognize academic credentials that whets students' appetites, and obliges teachers to succumb to examination pressures.

Whatever its other failures, and there are many, education is not responsible for the breakdown of school-leavers' transitions into working life. Later chapters explain that the failure responsible for the spread of youth unemployment has been overwhelmingly on the jobs side of the labour market. Young people are as able and willing to work as ever, but their jobs have gone. Whatever the educational regime, school-leavers would have floundered as unemployment rose beyond 3,000,000. During the recession firms have been reluctant, maybe unable, to maintain their side of school-leavers' former bridges into working life. Furthermore, as the next chapter explains, if there was any post-war neglect this occurred in industry where firms failed to create induction and training procedures that could withstand a prolonged recession.

3

Post-War Youth
in the Labour Market

Training and further education for all?

The end of World War II brought a period of all-round social and economic reconstruction. By 1950 Britain had a National Health Service, and a National Insurance system which promised security from cradle to grave. As the previous chapter explained, the 1944 Education Act decreed secondary education for all, and at the time there were equally radical proposals to offer a new deal to young people in employment.

The 1945 Ince Report envisaged sweeping youth unemployment and mis-employment into history by treating all beginning workers as trainees with opportunities to acquire vocational skills and prospects of career progression (Ministry of Labour and National Service, 1945). This report also advocated universal day release for general education and additional time off for vocational studies. These latter suggestions were not novel. Universal part-time education until age 18 was envisaged in the 1918 Education Act. However, like other Ince proposals, it has never been implemented.

The desirability of offering all school-leavers part-time further education has been endorsed by many subsequent committees and working parties. The 1959 Crowther Report affirmed the aspiration. So did the National Youth Employment Council in 1974. But in 1977, when formulating its proposals to deal with mounting youth unemployment, the MSC observed that two-thirds of all school-leavers still received no further education. Proposals for treating all beginning workers as trainees have met a similar fate. In 1978 the Assistant General Secretary of the TUC lamented that:

... our education and training systems between them currently consign about half the young people who enter employment each year to the category labelled 'no further investment required'. Could anyone really imagine that these young people are being properly equipped to make their way in a changing world? (Graham, 1978).

In 1981 the MSC proposed a New Training Initiative that promised training for all school-leavers. The idea is not new. Has its hour arrived?

Following the Ince Report, the government encouraged employers associations and trade unions to agree national apprenticeship systems for each industry and establish standards for training to meet. A few employers, including the Post Office, presumed that training and continuing education for all beginning workers would soon become normal if not mandatory and implemented the Ince philosophy, but throughout the greater part of industry apprenticeship was revived only in traditional craft occupations. By 1950, a third of male school-leavers and 8 per cent of girls were obtaining apprenticeships. These figures subsequently fluctuated without changing dramatically. In 1978–9, 37 per cent of boys' and 7 per cent of girls' first real jobs were apprenticeships (Careers Bulletin, 1982).

Post-war youth labour markets remained gender-divided. For girls apprentice training was unusual except in a handful of traditionally female trades such as hairdressing. However, throughout the 1950s and 1960s neither the girls themselves nor the wider society appeared to regard routine office, factory and shop jobs as other than sensible stop-gaps between school-leaving and motherhood. Women had already been emancipated, or so it was believed. The remaining gender differences were considered natural or socially necessary. Before World War II, even dead-end jobs were considered satisfactory for young single women; after the war, employers remained reluctant to train young women who were liable to 'swan off' and have children. Young female workers are often still expected to acquire occupational skills such as shorthand and typing in their own time at their own expense, while males are offered on-the-job training and day release (Ashton and Maguire, 1980a).

Day-release became a normal feature of apprenticeships and, during the initial post-war decade, the numbers of (mainly male) young workers benefiting increased. Technical college enrolments on National Certificate and City and Guilds courses expanded. However, the Crowther Report (1959) explained that few of the young people who enrolled actually earned qualifications. On National Certificate courses, only 16 per cent of students obtained the Ordinary, and a mere 6 per cent gained the Higher National award. On City and Guilds courses, 28 per cent obtained the Intermediate, and 6 per cent earned the Final Certificate.

Drop-out and failure rates were high. Research among students found that many apprentices treated day-release as a day off work (Venables, 1967). Most teachers of technical subjects are committed to offering 'useful' knowledge. They argue that 'relevance' is essential to motivate students. Nevertheless, the latter often complain that their education in classrooms and workshops is abstract, esoteric and unrelated to their jobs (Gleeson and Mardle, 1980). Many resent being sent back to school. The Crowther Committee recommended developing day-release as a universal right so that secondary and further education could be more closely integrated, and neither job changes nor employers' whims would interrupt young people's studies. In practice, however, enthusiasm for part-time further education waned. After the creation of CATs in 1956, then more so following the Robbins Report in 1963 and the designation of the new Polytechnics after 1966, full-time higher education became the leading growth area. From the 1950s until the introduction of the Youth Opportunities Programme in 1978, day-release ceased to be an educational growth sector.

Non-apprenticed youth

Young people who did not benefit from the post-war revival of apprenticeship were offered a new deal, as a result of a full employment and the changing occupational structure rather than by legislation or government measures. White-collar employment expanded. Girls with qualifications flooded into office jobs. Boys from the grammar and technical schools became trainees in the professions, management and in science and technology-based occupations.

The school-leaving age was raised to 15 in 1947. National Service was then in force, and these measures reduced the numbers of young people competing for employment. Keynesian economics and full-employment policies meant jobs for all school-leavers in most parts of the country. Instead of being surplus to requirements, beginning workers found their services in demand. School-leavers were courted by employers. Firms facing labour shortages made school-leavers a prime target. The quality as well as the supply of jobs for young workers improved. Employers found it impossible to fill dead-end vacancies. Tea girl and messenger boy jobs all but disappeared. To recruit school-leavers, employers had to offer either genuine training, or opportunities to advance rapidly towards adult earnings in non-skilled employment.

Young workers' wages rose more rapidly than other earnings, the affluent young worker was born and teenage consumers became a prime market for the leisure industries (Abrams, 1961). During the 1950s, the appearance of Teddy boys and rock 'n roll indicated that young people were using their newly-won economic power to establish a cultural independence. School-leavers who received neither further education nor training derived maximum benefit from these trends (Roberts, 1983). They were no longer trapped in low-paid blind alleys. Nor were they officially referred to as juveniles. The *Youth* Employment Service offered vocational advice and assistance in finding jobs, when necessary. Young workers went 'on board' early in their careers, and researchers began to unravel the inter-relationships between young people's treatment at home, their new status in the wider society, and their behaviour at work. An enquiry among young female piece-rate workers in an Irish clothing factory found that the girls' output correlated negatively with the proportions of their wages handed to parents (Bhroin, 1970). Millward's (1968) research among adolescent girls in three north-west factories also found that the workers became more industrious and productive when they began to 'board' and had a personal incentive to maximize their earnings. The 1959 Crowther Report on the education of 15–18 year olds noted and pondered the significance of post-war affluence. On the one hand, the long-term decline in fertility had created smaller, more prosperous families, better-placed than pre-war households to maintain their children in education. At the same time, higher wages were an inducement to forsake learning for earning at the earliest opportunity. This report also noted how young people's new-found affluence and independence were helping to erode respect for traditional authorities, thereby creating new discipline problems in schools.

Post-war public opinion did not adopt school-leavers as objects for sympathy. Young workers were not regarded as exploited or under-privileged. Older generations with pre-war memories suspected that post-war youth had it too easy. Employers expressed concern at their difficulties in persuading young people to undergo training and further education, and forgo the higher earnings immediately available else-where. Advocates of careers education and counselling argued that young people had a 'choice problem', and needed information and guidance to make sensible use of their opportunities. But there was another view of the situation; that society was having to cope with a 'youth problem'. Society's problem was how to persuade Teds, rockers and beatniks to take education, training and employment seriously. 'Problem groups' such as the handicapped, young people in depressed regions, the generally unsettled and delinquent, and racial minorities attracted periodic attention, but the majority of school-leavers did not appear to be suffering employment problems.

The old predictors of success continued to operate in post-war youth labour markets. Even physique remained relevant in the immediate post-war years. Ferguson and Cunnison's (1951, 1956) research among 14-year-olds who left Glasgow schools in February 1947 revealed that physical assessments, personality, academic attainments, fathers' occupations, family composition, and the status of the districts where individuals lived were related to their post-school fortunes. But these variables were no longer distinguishing those who obtained jobs from the unemployed. The main distinction in post-war Britain was between, on the one hand, entrants into white-collar jobs, apprenticeships and other occupations involving systematic training, and on the other, those who entered unskilled but nevertheless 'permanent', and often well-paid employment.

In relatively depressed regions including Merseyside and the north-east, youth (and adult) unemployment returned soon after the war, and persisted in the face of successive governments' economic and regional policies. But throughout the greater part of the country, even the abolition of National Service at the end of the 1950s, then the entry of 'the bulge' into the workforce from 1962–4, failed to revive mass youth unemployment. Geographers drew attention to how cities such as Bradford dominated by the textile industry, Stoke with its ceramics, and Barrow with shipbuilding and marine engineering, catered 'inefficiently for the wide range of potential talent of their inhabitants' (Rawstron and Coates, 1966). A small-scale but detailed study of school-leavers in London and Sunderland in 1971 demonstrated how, even when unemployment was avoided, young people's prospects varied with the prosperity of their regions. In London nearly all school-leavers seemed able to obtain a jobs compatible with their preferences. In Sunderland, in contrast, a half of those interviewed had to settle for jobs quite different from their ambitions (Murray and Orwell, 1972).

However, even in the depressed regions the majority of school-leavers were entering jobs that could be kept, rather than blind alleys. Among girls the main distinction was between those who aspired to and obtained office jobs, and the remainder who found work in factories and shops. Girls were rarely encouraged by parents and teachers to gain the necessary qualifications and seek training in 'masculine' trades. All the pressures on adolescent girls encouraged them to seek jobs in environments, preferably offices, where they could practise and maintain feminine appearances.

The great divide among boys who left school at the earliest opportunity was between apprentices and unskilled workers. All studies of school-leavers since World War II have confirmed the importance that boys attach to 'getting a trade'. Male youth were advised by parents with pre-war memories that trades meant security. Ryrie and Weir (1978) followed the progress of 182 Scottish school-leavers who entered engineering apprenticeships in 1972, and found that their subjects had sought trades because they wanted skilled and satisfying jobs with prospects rather than routine work, but, above all, for the security. While serving their time, some apprentices decided that, eventually, they would seek employment in other occupations. They had discovered that their trades would be neither as satisfying nor as well-paid as they had hoped. But even these apprentices had 'no regrets'. They believed that they would always be able to return to their trades, and that serving their time had delivered security.

Industrial training

In general, post-war researchers have not shared apprentices' own confidence in their training. Apprenticeship is a medieval institution. The 1512 Statute of Artificers made it the sole legal way of learning a trade. This Act was repealed in 1814, by which time it has ceased to be observed, but then, instead of withering, apprenticeship was revived in nineteenth-century industrial towns and factories. Employers adopted the institution, complete with indentures, as a method of training skilled workers and as a source of cheap labour, while the new craft unions began using apprenticeship like medieval guilds, to regulate entry into their occupations. Since 1945 successive governments have backed the apprentice system and training has become the prime objective, but other uses of the system by trade unions and employers have never disappeared.

Since World War II, researchers have repeatedly attacked apprenticeship on two main grounds (Williams, 1957; Liepmann, 1960). Firstly, they have argued that this method of vocational training, administered and financed by employers, sometimes subject to the consent of trade unions, consistently produces an under-trained and under-skilled workforce. Training is costly. Equipment and workshop space must be provided. Trainers must be paid, as well as trainees. Accommodating the latter can be organizationally inconvenient as well as expensive. Firms ensure that they do not train workers who will prove surplus to their own requirements. They certainly seek to avoid training competitors' workforces. Some decide that it is cheaper to poach than to train. Hence

Table 1   After compulsory schooling: UK, West Germany and France

	Full-time general education	Vocational education	Apprentice-ship	Work or unemployment
UK 1977	32	10	14	44
West Germany 1980	25	18	50	7
France 1978	27	40	14	19

Source: Manpower Services Commission (1981) A New Training Initiative: a consultative document, London. HMSO.

the persistent skill shortages that afflict British industry even during recessions.

The Ince proposal to treat all beginning workers as trainees was not based solely on concern for the young people's education and welfare. It recognized that occupational and technological trends were making it unrealistic to regard the labour force as divided into those with skills, and others who were required to contribute little more than muscle power. As the Ince Report envisaged, demand for completely unskilled labour has declined since 1945. Machines have replaced muscles. Simultaneously, crafts have been transferred from workers' hands into machines. As a result, rather than skilled and unkilled grades, it has become more realistic to think of the entire workforce as requiring skills, albeit of different degrees of complexity.

In 1981, when proposing its New Training Initiative, the MSC confirmed a generation of researchers' judgement: 'Training is not given sufficient priority in Britain'. The MSC (1982) estimated that by 1985 there would be more white than blue-collar workers and that completely unskilled jobs would continue to disappear. Britain's treatment of young people was judged grossly out-of-line with future labour requirements. In 1977, 44 per cent of all adolescents were still completing compulsory schooling, then receiving no further education or training. The MSC noted that Britain's main European competitors, France and West Germany, allowed only 19 and 7 per cent of their school-leavers to embark upon their careers with so little vocational preparation (see Table 1). Surveys among employers in Britain have found virtually unanimous agreement that more young people should be trained. Unfortunately, the employers also agree that training is too costly for their own enterprises to increase their efforts (Yates and Hall, 1982).

Young people have not been confined in life-long castes, depending upon whether they received training at the outset of their careers. Some individuals have descended the occupational hierarchy by abandoning

apprenticeships or when their skills became redundant, which has happened in many older, now declining industries such as shipbuilding.
Blue-collar workers are sometimes promoted to supervisory and management positions. Workers who never served apprenticeships are
sometimes upgraded following courses at MSC Skillcentres, or by 'dilution' when employers, faced with shortages of skilled workers, promote experienced employees. The fact that, since 1945, nearly a half of
all Britain's school-leavers have proceeded to neither further education
nor training has not condemned them all to lifetimes in unskilled jobs.
But lack of previous education and training has proved a handicap
whenever workers have been displaced. Individuals who move from
school to unskilled jobs, without acquiring any basic skills or technical
education, are not easily retrained. Employers regard them as poor risks.
They lack the basic vocational preparation on which to build. Hence the
British economy's persistent difficulties in adapting its workforce to
changing technologies.

A second set of criticisms concerns the quality of training offered to
apprentices. The inadequacies of on-the-job training, 'standing next to
Nellie', were well-publicized during the 1950s. Experienced workers are
not always competent teachers. Firm-based apprenticeships were also
criticized for introducing only the limited range of skills practised in
particular establishments. The inflexible age limits enshrined in many
apprenticeships systems, which made it necessary for young people to
leave school at the earliest opportunity to stand any chance of training,
and the rigid lengths, which bore no necessary relationship to the volume
and complexity of the skills, were condemned as wasteful. The manner
in which individuals became skilled purely by serving their time, without facing any test of competence or knowledge, was also deplored. The
difficulties of relating the on-the-job experience provided in different
firms to the 'theory' offered in further education, provoked further
criticism.

Apprentices themselves are aware of, and some complain about their
training's shortcomings. Many of Ryrie and Weir's (1978) apprentices
realized that their on-the-job experience lacked breadth, and resented
the many occasions when experienced craftsmen offered 'no explanation'. 'Success' has been difficult to measure since apprentices have never
faced uniform tests of competence, but Ryrie and Weir found that their
sample's achievements were not related to individuals' characteristics so
much as the training regimes. Systematic training programmes, containing clearly defined ranges and levels of skill, which explored the links
between college and workshop experience, appeared the most effective.
There have been numerous attempts to remedy the acknowledged

weaknesses in Britain's apprenticeship system. The 1958 Carr Report advised industries to establish better intelligence services to forecast future manpower needs. It recommended group schemes to widen trainees' experience, and mechanisms to share the costs of training throughout all firms that benefited. This report also called for definite training syllabuses, tests of skill, and a revision of age limits. Like previous and later attempts, the Carr Committee suggested curing the weaknesses by reforming rather than replacing the apprenticeship system. Following this report, the government attempted to promote reform by exhortation, which had little effect.

The 1964 Industrial Training Act recognized that exhortation had failed, and attempted to effect a training 'revolution' (Williams, 1969) by creating Industrial Training Boards which imposed levies then dispensed grants. The idea was to prompt firms to train enough workers to meet their industries' needs. In addition, the quality of training was to be enhanced. Boards were able to fix standards, and make grants conditional upon training covering stipulated skills, introduced in a coherent fashion. Under this regime, training became more systematic. Firms appointed Training Officers, and ensured that their provisions qualified for grants. But there was no increase in the proportion of young people entering apprenticeships. Before long, the training boards were under attack for burdening industry with their own costly bureaucracies and a flood of paperwork. Firms complained that training was being tailored to meet bureaucratic criteria rather than genuine needs, and campaigned for freedom to administer and finance training at their own properly informed discretion. During and since the 1970s, some training boards have been abolished. The powers to impose levies of those remaining are now restricted. Their principal role has become advisory—gathering intelligence and disseminating information about training needs and methods.

The 1973 Employment and Training Act did not tamper with training for beginning workers. This Act gave the MSC its statutory foundation. Subsequently the Department of Employment 'hived off' most of its employment services to this quango, after reaching agreement that the MSC would concentrate its activities among adult employees. Advising and placing young people in their initial jobs were not delegated to the MSC, but to a mandatory local authority Careers Service (formerly the Youth Employment Service), and prime responsibility for training beginning workers remained with industry.

In 1980 the Central Policy Review Staff found it necessary to repeat all the familiar criticisms of apprenticeship, and renew the call for the abolition of age limits and the introduction of tests of competence. These proposals were repeated in the MSC's 1981 New Training Initiative. By then the criticisms of apprenticeship were widely known and accepted by all political parties and all sides of industry. But are the obstacles to reform better understood today than in 1945?

Despite the many criticisms, traditional apprenticeship retains powerful support. Some researchers have argued that long initiations, regulated by employers and trade unions, allow recruits to assimilate their mentors' responsible attitudes and work habits as well as technical skill (Ryrie and Weir, 1978). Trade unions believe that the apprentice system enables them to exercise some control over numbers recruited as well as the content and practice of training. Employers find training expensive, but can mitigate the costs by their use of cheap apprentice labour, and can control training budgets by deciding how many apprentices to recruit. Industry has always resisted proposals to hand vocational training to any statutory agency. Firms have feared that such training methods would become expensive, and that governments would recoup the costs through levies or taxes on payrolls or profits. They have feared the creation of an independent training industry, growing under its own momentum, providing training and education unrelated to industry's needs, at crippling expense. Employers agree that if Britain is to have a successful economic future, more young people must be trained in new types of skills, to use new technologies and, above all, to be sufficiently flexible and adaptable to be able to apply generic skills to new tasks and master new techniques. But industry has never been prepared to finance and organize this training. In response to recruitment problems, firms have turned on education and demanded that schools and colleges offer vocational preparation free of charge to employers.

This is why traditional methods of assimilating young people into employment have survived despite persistent and substantiated criticism. If the Ince Report's proposals had been enacted, the rise of unemployment since the mid-1970s might have been less disastrous for Britain's youth. Their occupations would have been 'sheltered'. The principles of universal continuing education and training for all beginning workers have commanded general support since 1945, but while praising the end, industry has never been prepared to will the means.

Strain and turmoil?

Few school-leavers worry about whether sufficient numbers of their age group receive the quality of training to satisfy future skill requirements. Sixteen- year-olds worry about their own training and job opportunities. The wider issues have been raised by academics and government working parties. However, throughout the post-war years, the latter found a variety of reasons for suspecting that young people themselves were experiencing strain and stress during the transition into employment. To begin with, many beginning workers entered dull jobs without training or prospects. Were good wages (relative to adolescents' modest commitments) an adequate consolation? Secondly, young people had to step abruptly from school to the very different world of work. Thirdly, the majority made the transition in a state of vocational ignorance, uncertain of their objectives. Fourthly, many appeared to drift haphazardly into and between successive jobs indicating, perhaps, that they were disturbed and unable to adjust to employment.

This stress and strain view of abrupt transitions has recently been aired again, in an attempt to derive some consolation from the disappearance of school-leavers' real jobs. The new, prolonged transitions are said to be less traumatic. This is nonsense. All studies of post-war youth in the labour market found that the majority had little difficulty in handling their abrupt transitions. Researchers identified various reasons why school-leavers might have found the transition stressful, then proceeded to explain how and why the majority were able to cope.

Post-war researchers discovered that the most frequently named vocational reward that school-leavers claimed to seek was 'interesting work' (Sykes, 1953; Crowther Report, 1959; Hale, 1971). The media image of hedonistic youth working solely for money and living for Saturday nights has always been a misrepresentation. The majority of post-war school-leavers entered jobs involving some form of training and career progression. Some unskilled occupations were as secure as the businesses, allowing young people to settle as members of 'the family', to learn the ropes, become indispensable and carve their own careers. However, substantial numbers of post-war school-leavers were hired as cheap, *de facto* temporary labour by marginal businesses and some larger companies including supermarkets, which staffed permanent jobs with streams of transitory young workers. The employers realized that the terms and conditions of work would not attract permanent employees.

Throughout the full-employment decades, job mobility rates were high among young unskilled workers. In their initial three years in the workforce, Ferguson and Cunnison's (1951) Glasgow school-leavers held an average of 2.77 different jobs. In Carter's (1962) Sheffield study, 60 per cent of the young people changed jobs during their initial six months. Maizels (1970) did not find the rate of job changing in her subsequent London enquiry surprising. She considered most of the jobs unsuitable for young people:

> Since few occupations allow for the full use of talents, while a large proportion of jobs for adolescents, as adults, require little technical or other skill, any match achieved is minimal. In many cases it depends on the capacity of the individual to modify his inclinations, and to function with many of his known and unknown talents dormant. (p. 273)

Maizels argued that '. . . the present requirements of the economic and social structure conflict with the needs of young adolescents to develop and assert their true individuality' (p. 319), and called for planned opportunities for all beginning workers to sample a range of jobs, day-release and promotion prospects for all, so as to make early work experience truly educational. Other investigators echoed these sentiments. Carter (1966) recommended job enlargement, universal part-time education and continuing guidance. Ashton and Field (1976) called for the abolition of careerless employment.

Young people had to cope with a sudden transition from communities designed to cater for their physical and psychological needs, where they enjoyed the companionship of peers, organized games, health and cultural facilities. They faced longer working hours, shorter holidays, amoral supervisors and workmates. Instead of progressive syllabuses many were expected to learn routine tasks, then repeat them, *ad infinitum*. Wartime research had drawn attention to 14-year-olds' difficulties in adjusting to long hours in repetitive jobs. Tenen (1947a, 1947b) studied young workers in two clothing factories, explained how the working conditions were poor compared with schools, and how the former school seniors found it difficult to come to terms with their instant transformation into the most junior employees. The girls had eagerly anticipated starting work: it promised adventure, status and a fresh start. Then on entering industry they encountered arduous hours, menial jobs and treatment as juveniles. The beginning workers had been accustomed to playtimes and engineered them at work, to their supervisors' annoyance. A stream of post-war writers argued that young workers needed coaches, counsellors, youth workers or sympathetic supervisors to ease the transition (King George's Jubilee Trust, 1955).

Researchers explained how school-leavers approached the transition with minimal preparation. The previous chapter noted how education has been criticized for neglecting careers guidance. Interviews with final-year pupils identified many who found starting work a source of worry, which they faced alone (Hill and Scharff, 1976). Anderson (1976) drew attention to how 'the child in an industrial, urban society is set in an artificial situation, preparing for a life at work, but having no real contact with work'. Carter (1962) described how the majority of his Sheffield school-leavers embarked upon their working lives in a state of vocational ignorance, uncertain of what they would like to do. Neither parents nor teachers were sufficiently informed to offer comprehensive advice, though the formers' attitudes were often influential. Careers teachers and officers made little impression. Homes and schools tended to shield young people from the world of work until the day arrived when they were plunged in. School-leavers' occupational choices were often notional, at best provisional, sometimes invented purely to satisfy the enquiries of teachers, careers officers and researchers (Ryrie and Weir, 1978).

Finally, all the relevant enquiries found many school-leavers drifting into and out of their early jobs in an apparently haphazard manner. Approximately a third of first jobs and a smaller proportion of subsequent occupations were obtained through the statutory agencies. These 'low' figures drew criticism, but compared with official agencies in other countries the British Careers Service has an outstanding record (Reubens, 1977). Needless to say, the spread of youth unemployment since the mid-1970s has led to even greater contact with the Careers Service. Young people must register to claim social security and to gain access to special measures. Unemployment has also inhibited job-changing. In the late 1970s a Youthaid inquiry (1979) found that, 18 months into their working lives, 81 per cent of a nation-wide sample had held no more than two jobs.

Approximately a third of school-leavers obtained their first jobs through parents and relatives. Being 'spoken for' is still an important route into apprenticeships. In Carter's (1962) study, many parents and young people regarded the (then) Youth Employment Service as a 'last resort', to be used only if informal networks failed. It has always appeared strange to some observers that while young people are in education, preparing for their future careers, it is considered important to minimize the influence of—and ensure that pupils are not disadvantaged by—their home backgrounds, whereas, at the point of entering employment, school-leavers' fates are left heavily dependent upon family contacts.

Some of the remaining school-leavers learnt about their jobs from adverts and teachers, but all enquiries noted that many located employment through off-chance enquiries at local factories, shops and offices. Which occupations these young people entered seemed to depend mainly on chance. Exactly how many school-leavers obtained jobs consistent with their stated ambitions varied from area to area depending on the quantity and breadth of local opportunities. In Carter's (1962) Sheffield study only a quarter of the school-leavers were successful with their first applications, whereas in Maizels' (1970) London inquiry a half of the boys and two-thirds of the girls obtained the first jobs they applied for. The ease with which young people found jobs also depended upon their qualifications, family contacts and personalities. Individuals who are self-assured, forthcoming and co-operative in interviews have always found the search for work relatively simple, even in periods of high unemployment (Lazarsfeld and Gaudet, 1941). But throughout the post-war years, all school-leavers' prospects seemed to owe a great deal to chance—who their parents knew, and which jobs they heard about through grapevines. Researchers' inability to fully explain school-leavers' occupational destinies by manipulating independent variables has never been entirely due to the 'noise' generated by insensitive research instruments. Pure luck, being in the right place at the right time, has always played an important role during the transition into employment, and in subsequent job-changing.

The awaiting jobs, the abrupt transition and haphazard job-searching that could not ensure the best fit between school-leavers' aspirations, capacities and the available employment, impressed some commentators as grounds for portraying the transition as a period of stress and turmoil, like other aspects of adolescence. Writers who took this view endeavoured to make young people's problems visible, hoping to provoke parents, teachers, careers workers and politicians to demand a better deal for beginning workers. However, the wider society was unimpressed. Employers appeared willing to operate existing procedures. Young people themselves were not complaining.

The previous chapter explained how, prior to school-leaving, most young people have been keen, sometimes desperately keen to be released, to become wage-earning adults. Recent school-leavers have worried less about the transition into employment than the possibility of remaining jobless (Youthaid, 1979). Once in employment, the overwhelming majority have expressed satisfaction with their occupations. No post-war inquiry found more than 10 per cent confessing dissatisfaction. Some researchers hesitated before accepting this picture of contentment at face value. What do individuals mean when they claim job satisfaction? Do they find their work satisfying or just satisfactory? What are their yardsticks: their ideal occupations, or merely the other jobs they might have entered? Are young and older workers inhibited from criticizing jobs that they are credited with having chosen?

Other investigators believed their own evidence, took young people's professed satisfaction seriously, and set about explaining why, despite the possible stresses, the majority made smooth transitions. The main explanations fall under two complementary headings: anticipatory socialization and occupational socialization.

Anticipatory socialization

School-leavers' apparent lack of vocational information, advice and guidance was deceptive. Teachers rarely offered detailed advice. Deliberate careers teaching was spasmodic and ineffective. Nevertheless, as the previous chapter explained, 'careers' has always been an important aspect of education's hidden curriculum. Selection within education has accustomed young people to their awaiting positions in the job hierarchy. Parents are rarely able to dispense comprehensive information about national or even local labour markets, but children become familiar with their attitudes towards work and, as a result, know roughly what to expect.

In the past, the majority of young people travelled along well-signposted trajectories. Their home backgrounds and educational streams enabled them to anticipate their initial occupations and the types of adult employment to which these early jobs would lead. Although unsure of which particular occupations they would prefer, the majority were realistic about their levels of employment. In Hargreaves' (1967) study of fourth-form secondary modern school boys, 93 per cent in the A stream, but only 41 per cent in the D stream entertained hopes of apprenticeships or non-manual jobs. Before entering employment, young people have grown accustomed to making 'realistic' educational choices. Most secondary school pupils can be relied upon to make 'sensible' decisions about whether to enter 'O'-levels, CSEs or attempt both because they have already internalised the educational system's view of their abilities and the appropriateness of different courses for different pupils (Woods, 1976; Ryrie, Furst and Lauder, 1979).

Beginning workers have always faced problems of adjustment. On entering employment they have needed to learn technical and social skills, and adjust to new daily routines. But the overwhelming majority have proved that they are capable of these adjustments. Problems with workmates, bosses and coping with the longer working day have usually been resolved within weeks (Palmer, 1964). In most cases, when jobs were available, there was no clash between the new demands to which beginning workers were exposed, and the latter's aspirations and self-images (Ashton and Field, 1976).

School-leavers' inability to specify exactly which occupations they wished to enter could be construed as further evidence of realism. Aspiring apprentices learnt from parents that the important thing is to 'get a trade' and that which trade was of secondary importance. School-leavers who saw their futures in office, shop and factory work knew that which particular job hardly mattered. They did not expect their initial occupations to last for life. They realized that the pros and cons of the different jobs they might be offered would probably be self-cancelling. All this was known as a result of assimilating the attitudes of parents and neighbours. Advice to 'think carefully' was often dismissed as another illustration of teachers' idiocy (Willis, 1977).

Haphazard job-hunting can be less irrational than it appears. Advice from relatives and neighbours who have worked in local firms may be superior to careers information in manuals and job descriptions at careers offices. Most school-leavers expect (and indeed, insist upon) finding work locally—certainly no more than a single bus ride from their homes. They cannot afford long-distance commuting, and they would not dream of uprooting themselves, leaving friends and families, for mere jobs. After all, the majority leave school seeking jobs, not careers. They expect to find work within local labour markets that can be scoured by off-chance enquiries, assisted by information and advice through grapevines.

Rather than indicating that young unskilled workers were unable to settle, their frequent job changing could be interpreted as a rational use of limited opportunities (Roberts, 1981a). Individuals moved to obtain pay increases, to reduce travelling costs and, sometimes, simply to relieve the tedium of any one job. Mobility may not damage young unskilled workers' career prospects. It can widen their experience and accustom them to the adjustments the majority have to make repeatedly during their working lives. Some employers use young people as cheap dispensable labour, and post-war school-leavers used these 'trash jobs' to build the experience that equipped them, in time, to compete for employment in firms offering better wages, conditions, security and even career prospects.

Occupational socialization

Sceptics who refused to believe that post-war transitions were as smooth as their surface appearances, were making the same mistake as more recent critics who have used the return of youth unemployment to indict education. The mistake is applying an unrealistic yardstick in assessing school-leavers' preparation for the transition. It is unrealistic to expect school-leavers to enter the labour market with comprehensive knowledge of occupations, certain of their preferences, to search for jobs systematically and settle immediately in the occupations to which they are best suited. Beginning workers will always lack knowledge of occupations and their own potential. The initial stages of working life must be a period of exploration and self-discovery. Homes and schools cannot solve, but they can equip beginning workers to cope with these problems, and post-war history proved that the majority could cope. While the employment side of school-leavers' bridges remained intact, learning at work was able to take over from anticipatory socialization.

Once in employment, individuals are exposed to occupational cultures within which they discover the rewards their jobs can offer. Those who are sufficiently impressed, remain, learn to value the rewards, and sometimes develop self-concepts, views of their own talents and preferences, even entire life styles that make the types of work they have entered feel perfect niches. Once individuals' occupations and self-concepts become interwoven, the involuntary loss of a job can be psychologically debilitating (Hughes, 1951).

Occupational socialization is most easily illustrated, and has been studied most frequently in professions such as medicine, nursing and engineering where recruitment and training are arranged in clear stages (Merton, Reader and Kendall, 1957; Becker and Carper, 1956a and 1956b; Becker et al, 1963; Simpson, 1979). Novices learn technical skills and, in the process, build occupational identities. By the end of their training, medical students are no longer acting a part; they *are* doctors. Professions are not typical occupations, but similar on-the-job socialization has been observed among apprentice electricians, printers, hairdressers and business machine operators (Geer, 1972; Flude, 1977; Reimer, 1977). As recruits acquire craft knowledge they simultaneously develop pride in their skills. Instructors communicate characteristic attitudes and etiquettes, which trainees encourage each other to emulate.

Many post-war school-leavers failed to obtain their first-choice jobs, but the majority found employment on their preferred levels. Their fluid, provisional aspirations meant that most school-leavers were flexible, and prepared to apply for, then accept, offers from a range of jobs

(Roberts, 1968a, 1968b). In most engagements, job applicants and employers have to make decisions with incomplete knowledge of the other party. Employers cannot hope to amass full knowledge of every applicant, any more than beginning workers can learn every relevant fact about all the jobs for which they could apply. Young people's choices and employers' decisions are inevitably provisional, but both parties have been able to cope with the uncertainty (Waddington, 1982). Following engagement, each side assesses the other, and re-evaluates their initial decisions. Job changing can be educational for young people, and profitable for employers.

No-one has ever suggested that all employees, including car assemblers and shop assistants, eventually settle in and identify with their occupations in the same way as medical students. Sometimes recruits learn to identify with employing organizations rather than occupations. A study in an English steelworks, before nationalization, found that only 27 per cent of apprentices expected to remain with the firm indefinitely (Scott *et al.*, 1956). Others hoped to move on, broaden their experience, practise their skills elsewhere and, in some cases, escape from the scene of early mistakes. In contrast, 68 per cent of the young labourers had no intention of leaving the employer—the largest firm, offering more attractive wages, greater security and other benefits than most local enterprises. Some workers build organizational rather than occupational careers, acquiring experience and skills which are valuable and confer status only while they remain with the one employer.

In some occupations recruits learn to value extrinsic rather than intrinsic rewards. Occupational survival sometimes depends on practitioners distancing their real selves from the job itself. Taxi-dancers (girls who sell their company on dance floors) must learn to feign romance and tolerate sexual advances yet remain 'straight'. Colleagues convince each other that all jobs and men are just the same, and thereby neutralize the occupation's demands (Hong and Duff, 1977). Males entering unskilled manual jobs have often graduated from school counter-cultures to shop-floor cultures where they enjoy solidaristic peer relationships and the daily battle of wits with management rather than their actual work tasks (Willis, 1977).

The details vary from occupation to occupation and, to some extent, from person to person, but 'work establishment' always involves learning technical skills and, simultaneously, developing aspirations and self concepts that are congruent with the jobs. This is how young workers settled in the industrial labour force when jobs were plentiful. Some become tied to their occupations by positively identifying with the skills. In some jobs, the main ties were formed by building 'something to lose' that amounted to the most marginal advantage over newcomers' wages, less arduous jobs, longer holidays and/or sick pay, but having earned these perks, workers are reluctant to place them at risk by deserting their careers (Freedman, 1969; Krause, 1971; Mann, 1973). Many beginning workers spent their early working lives 'milling around', taking numerous short-lived jobs, often in small firms that were unable to offer any prospects, until their age and experience enabled the employees to enter organizations and occupations within which it was possible to build careers by proving their competence in a range of tasks, edging their earnings upwards in the process.

The decay of clear roads

Smooth transitions from education to adult occupations were never universal. There were always casualties. Researchers identified a minority of chronic job-changers who seemed unable to settle in any occupation, who were permanently 'at odds' (Department of Employment, 1970; Baxter, 1975). Sometimes the young people's inability to settle was a symptom of deeper socio-psychological disturbance: work was just one of many situations to which they were unable to adjust (Logan and Goldberg, 1954; Wilkins, 1955). In other instances, individuals were unable to find occupations compatible with firm aspirations and self-concepts they had developed during childhood. Career progress was sometimes disrupted by economic and technological change. But throughout the 1950s and 1960s there was sufficient consistency between school-leavers' ambitions and the occupational structure for the majority to make smooth transitions. This is why there was no powerful grass-roots demand for a restructuring of work entry. The main problems surrounding work entry were never transitional, so much as rooted in the quality of the available jobs. Too many of the niches in which young people settled offered insufficient training and prospects for the economy's good. There were indications during the full employment years that casualty rates were increasing as a result of the long-term trends identified in Chapter 1. First, the occupational structure was changing. The proportion of jobs in manufacturing, particularly unskilled jobs, was declining, whereas the proportions of young people surviving the 16-plus then continuing in education to earn advanced qualifications, and obtaining apprenticeships were stable. In the long run, these trends would have left 16-year-old school-leavers competing for a slowly diminishing number of 'ordinary' jobs. Increasing numbers who obtained 'youth jobs' would have lacked the qualifications and training to move to adult occupations within which they could build at least modest careers.

Secondly, school-leavers were changing—they were becoming more ambitious. Industrial and urban change were slowly undermining the status-assenting working-class communities where sons followed fathers, daughters followed mothers and destinies were scripted by tradition. Simultaneously, schools were encouraging more and more young people to acquire (modest) qualifications. By the 1960s in some parts of Britain, homes and schools had ceased reproducing a stratum of young people who were content to build careers in unskilled jobs (Roberts, Duggan and Noble, 1981). These occupations were filled by labour from the Caribbean and Indian sub-continent, and by recruiting women, 'green' from their homes. By the 1970s females and ethnic minorities were protesting and sometimes resisting this subordination. There was less conflict between school-leavers' ambitions and long-term occupational trends than between both and the employment offered to young people.

The slow decomposition of school-leavers' clear roads and smooth transitions would have continued, leaving increasing numbers of casualties until the transition itself became defined as 'a problem', but during the 1970s the slow decay became a collapse with the return of mass youth unemployment.

4

Mass Unemployment Returns

The spread of joblessness

The oil price spirals of the 1970s created world-wide inflation. Governments responded by plunging the entire western economy into recession. In Britain, output and employment in manufacturing declined sharply. In 1981–82 production was no higher than during the three-day week enforced by the 1973–74 coal-miners strike. Public spending and consequently the growth of service sector employment were restrained in 1976. These restraints were intensified under the 1979 Conservative government's monetarist policies. Throughout the 1970s the labour force was growing due to the long-term inflow of married women and increasing numbers of school-leavers, the consequence of a rising birth-rate from 1955 to 1965. A net loss of jobs coupled with increasing numbers seeking work sent unemployment soaring more rapidly than ever before in Britain's history, to over 3,000,000 in 1982.

The initial rise of unemployment was accompanied by debate as to whether involuntary joblessness was really spreading as rapidly as the statistics suggested. Were redundancy payments and earnings-related benefits enabling the unemployed to delay and search for the right jobs instead of settling for whatever was immediately available? Had the separation of social security claims from the Jobcentre service eased former pressures on claimants to apply for notified vacancies? (Layard, 1979). There were suggestions that employment protection legislation might have destroyed jobs by making employers reluctant to hire. However, by the time unemployment had reached 2,000,000 no-one believed that the above influences were more than marginal. The folklore of work-shy scroungers was easily ridiculed. The plain fact was that Britain had many more would-be workers than jobs.

During the 1980s, 3,000,000 out-of-work has invited comparison with the 1930s. There are many similarities, including some social and personal consequences of prolonged joblessness, but there are also important differences (Tomlinson, 1982). Firstly, Britain in the 1980s is faring worse, not better than her competitors. Opinions differ, needless to say, on whether this is due to the incompetence of the 1980s governments or to the low productivity, investment and profit margins, coupled with high inflation inherited from previous administrations.

Secondly, unemployment in the 1980s is a national malaise, less concentrated within severely depressed regions than in the 1930s. Unemployment is still well above average in regions dependent on older manufacturing industries like shipbuilding and textiles, vulnerable to international competition and technological change, and now in decline. But some growth industries of the 1950s including steel and motor vehicles have joined the older industries in shedding labour. Areas in the West Midlands, recently a boom region, have become industrial wastelands. In the still relatively prosperous south-east, unemployment blackspots have appeared, many in inner cities where the natural decline of older industries has been accelerated by urban re-development. The intention was to improve the environment. The consequences have often included the spread of social and economic blight. However, unemployment blackspots are not all close to city centres. During the 1970s and 1980s many of the 1950s new industrial estates, built for that generation's expanding industries, have been devastated by factory closures, creating extremely high unemployment in adjacent housing areas.

Thirdly, the 1980s unemployment is more concentrated among vulnerable groups, especially the unskilled and young people. Between 1972 and 1977 general unemployment rose by 45 per cent, and unemployment among 16–17-year-olds by 120 per cent. In 1977 there were 1,500,000 unemployed, 6 per cent of the workforce, but the unemployment rate for 16–18-year-olds was 8.8 per cent. In some regions it was considerably higher: 12.4 per cent on Merseyside, and in blackspots such as Knowsley (which includes Kirkby) it was 37.1 per cent. After 1977, despite the rapid expansion of special measures, the gap between youth and adult unemployment continued to widen. In October 1982, with general unemployment at 13.5 per cent, the rate for 16–19-year-olds was 28 per cent (see Table 2). Programmes to alleviate youth unemployment seemed to be waging a despairing battle against economic tides.

During the 1930s unemployment among young people was higher than for the adult workforce, but the gap was narrower than opened in the 1970s. In their 1910 survey of York, Rowntree and Lasker (1911) were surprised to find as many as 12.4 per cent of the 14–18-year-olds unemployed for over six months. It was believed at the time that school-leavers found jobs relatively easily, albeit juvenile jobs with low

Table 2 Unemployment rates by age-group: Great Britain, October 1982

	Males	*Females*	*Total*
Under 18	24.9	32.1	27.6
18–19	29.9	25.4	27.8
20–24	22.5	16.8	20.1
25–34	14.5	9.7	12.7
35–44	11.5	5.1	9.1
45–54	11.0	5.1	8.5
55–59	13.3	5.9	10.4
60+	20.5	0.7	15.5
All ages	16.0	10.0	13.5

pay, and that their risks of unemployment were greatest as blind alleys closed around age 18, when they became eligible for adult rates. This older pattern may be reappearing in the 1980s, with government policies having held down school-leavers' wage levels making them more attractive to employers, and with training and educational schemes aimed primarily at 16-year-old school-leavers. During the early 1980s joblessness began to spread rapidly among 20–24-year-olds, to 20 per cent in October 1982, but throughout the rise of unemployment towards 3,000,000, teenagers suffered more acutely than any other age groups.

Why have young people's jobs disappeared?

The recession of the 1970s and 1980s has victimized young people in three ways. First, when firms trim workforces, recruitment is reduced or halted, which is particularly frustrating for newcomers to the labour market, like school-leavers. Natural wastage can sound a painless way of shedding labour. It is less likely to encounter trade union opposition than redundancies. Existing workers are protected, but individuals without jobs, including school-leavers, are penalized when vacancies dry up.

Second, when profit margins are squeezed, training is often one of the 'luxuries' to be pruned. Firms realize that this economy threatens their long-term prospects, but when short-term survival is at risk all possible cutbacks are considered. In the 1960s 40 per cent of males leaving school at 16 or earlier were apprenticed. By 1980 this proportion had been halved. In 1968 there were 236,000 apprentices in manufacturing industry, but only 100,000 in 1982 (Manpower Services Commission, 1982).

Third, when general unemployment is high, young job seekers face strong competition from older experienced workers. Some school-leavers' jobs, including apprenticeships, are 'sheltered' because adults are ineligible. Other jobs are closed to young people who are considered immature and irresponsible, unsuited to heavy work, excluded by health, safety and other protective legislation, or because alcohol, driving and/ or shifts are involved. The majority of jobs open to young people are also open to adults, and the latter often win the favour of employers, many of whom, as previous chapters explained, have become highly critical of school-leavers (National Youth Employment Council, 1974; Colledge, Llewellyn and Ward, 1977).

We have seen that some employers' complaints are at variance with the facts. On any assessment, educational standards have risen. Studies that have recorded the usual complaints when employers were questioned about young people in general have found the same firms expressing complete satisfaction with their own young workers (Yates and Hall, 1982; Ashton, Maguire and Garland, 1982). Employers' criticisms may sometimes be attempts to disclaim responsibility for denying young people employment, but whatever firms' motives and however unjustified some may appear, the removal of unskilled manual jobs from youth labour markets seems to be a long-term trend that was accentuated, not instigated by the onset of recession in the mid-1970s. Throughout the 1960s, there was a decline in demand for unskilled teenagers, which more than offset the trend towards 'staying on' at school, and raising the school-leaving age in 1973 (National Youth Employment Council, 1974). Larger companies with scope for choice began restricting recruitment to semi and unskilled jobs to the over-18s, or even over-21s. New technologies which allow few opportunities for school-leavers to learn the ropes, the fact that teenagers had ceased to be cheap, market pressures on firms to reduce labour costs, the spread of shift systems, now covering over a third of male manufacturing jobs and the availability of cheap, part-time female labour could have been responsible. Whatever employers' motives, the 1970s recession accelerated the withdrawal of school-leavers' jobs.

Local labour markets

Beginning workers do not face equal risks of unemployment. Individuals' prospects depend not on national or even regional rates, but on the levels of unemployment in local labour markets, the areas within which, for practical purposes, their search for work is confined. The geographical shape and size of school-leavers' labour markets depends, among other things, on public transport networks. City centres are usually accessible from all suburbs whereas public transport to adjacent out-lying districts may be inconvenient. A Youthaid (1979) study of 250 school-leavers in London, Northumberland and Newcastle-upon-Tyne found that the average distance travelled to work was under 3 miles. Public transport is expensive. Teenagers cannot afford to commute long distances on the wages they are likely to be offered, unless their families are able and willing to subsidize the young people's employment. This is one reason why levels of youth unemployment can vary considerably within regions, even within the same towns and cities, and how young people in out-lying towns, villages and rural areas become trapped in local labour markets offering very limited opportunities. Acquiring a car or motor bike widens individuals' employment prospects, but once again, unless they have prosperous and generous parents, school-leavers and the young unemployed can rarely afford these assets. Once young adults have been able to save and purchase private transport, they can seek jobs further afield, and which involve starting and finishing work at unsocial hours. This is one way in which individuals escape from the 'trash jobs' paying 'slave wages' to which many school-leavers are confined.

Only nine respondents in the Youthaid study moved away from home in their search for work. Six of these entered the armed forces. Residential mobility is not a real option for most school-leavers unless they wish to join and are accepted by the armed services or in other occupations like nursing where accommodation is normally available along with the job. Beginning workers cannot afford independent flats and houses. Giving young people access to the national labour market will require the provision of cheap housing for all young single persons, not just full-time higher education students.

Qualifications

Within local labour markets, school-leavers' chances of gaining employment invariably depend upon their qualifications. Rising unemployment has implications for all beginning workers including university graduates. The latter have found their scope for choice narrowing. Instead of deciding which jobs to accept, many have been obliged to take whatever is offered. Instead of fixing jobs prior to graduation, some have remained unemployed for months, and have then been obliged to take temporary stop-gap vacancies. But graduates rarely become long-term unemployed. They can always move down the labour market if necessary, into formerly non-graduate occupations like local government, banking and insurance. There are now more graduate recruits into the executive than administrative civil service grades. Trading down occurs at all levels. In most parts of the country, 'O'-levels are now demanded for craft apprenticeships. It is school-leavers without useful qualifications, who would have obtained unskilled jobs in the relatively buoyant labour markets of the 1960s and who have nowhere downwards to trade, who tend to be left without any jobs. A 1977 national survey found that 53 per cent of the young unemployed had no qualifications, at a time when only a fifth of young people left school in this condition (Colledge *et al.*, 1977).

The most modest qualifications can enhance school-leavers' prospects. At the same time, even 'A'-levels and degrees carry no guarantee. There are no jobs where recruitment is wholly on the basis of educational attainments. When employers pay attention to qualifications, they invariably use additional criteria, including personal qualities such as maturity and appearing keen to work (Ashton *et al.*, 1982). Moreover, the value of a given level of qualification depends on the state of the labour market in which it is traded. When jobs were plentiful, CSEs enabled school-leavers to enter office jobs and apprenticeships. When the level of unemployment means that there are always better-qualified applicants even for unskilled jobs, lower-grade CSEs cease to be useful. This is why experiences and opinions among teachers and young people differ so sharply on the value of paper credentials.

Furthermore, a given level of qualification can enhance a group of school-leavers' prospects without being any use whatsoever to most members. Two CSEs rather than no qualifications may mean that 20 rather than 10 per cent of male school-leavers obtain craft apprenticeships or avoid joblessness completely, depending on the state of the local labour market. In either event, 80 per cent find that their qualifications are 'no use'. Teachers who advise pupils that qualifications will strengthen their chances in the labour market are telling the truth. At the same time they are increasing the likelihood of the young people finding cause to complain of 'broken promises'.

Pupils and parents react in diverse ways, depending on their predispositions, as unemployment devalues qualifications. The standard advice offered by middle-class and other aspiring parents is to 'try even harder'. Young people who take this advice battle on, sometimes as 'new sixth formers' and equip themselves with additional CSEs, 'O'-levels, and sometimes 'A'-levels before entering the labour market. These tactics are sometimes successful, but risky. Qualifications do not always carry the same weight at age 18 as at 16. 'Staying on' can make modestly qualified school-leavers too old for craft apprenticeships (Lee and Wrench, 1981).

Among young people from unskilled working class homes, a more common reaction to unemployment appears to be that 'even qualifications are no use'. Teachers are unable to motivate these pupils with the threat of unemployment and the carrot of qualifications. In districts where these attitudes are widespread, unemployment makes schooling seem more pointless, and teaching a more thankless task then ever. Pupils become restless, disillusioned and indifferent, when they are in attendance. It has been suggested that for these young people truanting can be a useful preparation for street life on the dole (Adams and Sawdon, 1978).

Contacts

In addition to their places of residence and qualifications, school-leavers' prospects depend upon their contacts. Informal job-finding and recruitment are as widespread as ever. Being 'spoken for' is still an advantage, and often decisive when seeking a good job. This applies at all levels of employment. Social class origins are irrelevant to students' performances within higher education, but discriminate at the point of entering the workforce. Graduates from middle-class homes are advised when and how to apply for jobs in prestigious professions such as law and accountancy (Kelsall *et al.*, 1972). Offering the right references, displaying a recognized school tie, speaking in the interviewer's accent and already being known by the right people add weight to job applications.

Equivalent processes operate in the competition for craft apprenticeships and, indeed, all 'worthwhile' jobs. Many young people who are left jobless, particularly the long-term unemployed, owe this fate to lacking useful contacts. In 1977, when youth unemployment was rising rapidly, an MSC survey found that 19 per cent of the young unemployed came from families with other members out of work, at a time when adult unemployment was 6 per cent, and 79 per cent had unemployed friends when unemployment among 16–18-year-olds was 8.8 per cent (Colledge *et al.*, 1977). The long-term young unemployed are concentrated in families and communities whose members are not the 'right people'. Some social backgrounds act as millstones: 'No-one from Liverpool 8 need apply' (Wilson and Womersley, 1977).

Research among the young unemployed has clarified how labour markets operate and how contacts work. Large firms' existing workforces are said to function as 'internal labour markets'. Competition for firms' better jobs is often limited to existing employees. These internal labour markets become 'extended' to non-employees with contacts that make them potential recruits (Manwaring, 1982). The barriers that divide potential recruits from other individuals may be invisible but they are extremely powerful. Within localities, these barriers segment all workers, in employment and jobless, into numerous labour markets, divided vertically and horizontally (Ashton and Maguire, 1982).

Why do large, otherwise highly bureaucratized enterprises persist with informal recruitment? It is inexpensive. The costs of placing and replying to adverts are avoided. It enables local managements to respond flexibly to novel problems and opportunities. Most important of all, firms discover that informal recruitment 'works' (Keil *et al.*, 1972). It enables them to exclude the 'unacceptable' and recruit non-troublesome labour (Jenkins, 1982). The costs are borne by individuals who would be competent but lack contacts. Young people from unskilled homes and the ethnic minorities (Lee and Wrench, 1981) are often trapped in this situation, excluded from the better jobs, and confined to 'slave labour', government schemes and unemployment.

Ethnic minorities

Every study to compare their prospects has found that black and brown school-leavers are less successful than whites in the quality of jobs obtained and avoiding unemployment (Allen and Smith, 1975; Brooks and Singh, 1978; Manchester City Council Planning Department, 1979; Ipswich National Union of Teachers Working Party, 1979; Watts, 1980; Dex, 1982). Unemployment among young people of West Indian origin, the most frequently researched minority, is two to three times as high as among whites.

Discrimination in the labour market is not the sole explanation. Racial disadvantage is multi-dimensional. Britain's non-white minorities are concentrated in high unemployment, inner-urban areas. The first generation immigrants settled in these 'twilight' districts where the majority have remained. Economic and cultural barriers have impeded their dispersal. West Indian pupils, but not Asians, under-achieve at school compared with the white population (Swann Report, 1981). Young people from all minority backgrounds tend to lack the contacts that facilitate entry into apprenticeships and other jobs worth keeping (Lee and Wrench, 1981). Asian youth sometimes retreat into family businesses, a course which is usually considered second-best (Fowler, Littlewood and Madigan, 1977). Entrepreneurial activity has been less common within West Indian communities; their young people often retreat into unemployment.

Discrimination in the labour market is piled on top of other racial disadvantages. Before 1968, discrimination was blatant and widespread. 'Coloureds' were excluded or subject to quotas in many firms. The 1968 Race Relations Act, strengthened in 1976, has made discrimination illegal, but the practice persists. Studies of identically qualified applicants for the same jobs always find that, overall, blacks are less successful than whites (Smith, 1977). Individual acts of discrimination are difficult to prove. Non-white youth may not always realize when they are being victimized (Allen and Smith, 1975). The thin stream of complaints reaching the Commission for Racial Equality (CRE) is evidence that existing legislation simply does not work, rather than that the law has changed behaviour. Immigration has not been a cause of rising unemployment. Since the 1960s the inflow has been reduced to a trickle, exceeded by emigration. The ethnic minorities who filled Britain's labour shortages during the 1950s and 1960s have simply borne the costs of subsequent economic failures.

On paper the battery of government-sponsored measures to achieve parity of treatment appears formidable. In addition to enforcing statutes forbidding discrimination, the CRE, supported by the Race Relations Employment Advisory Service within the Department of Employment, plays an educational role. Inner-city programmes and, insofar as they are aimed at disadvantaged groups, the MSC's training schemes for young people and adults, are intended to benefit ethnic minorites. Race relations is now covered in the initial training of all teachers and careers officers. Special language classes are offered in schools and further education. The MSC supports language training at places of employment. Yet despite all these measures, the spread of unemployment has been particularly rapid among ethnic minority youth. Between 1973 and 1976, when youth unemployment was creeping upwards, the proportion of ethnic minority youth among the young jobless rose from 2.8 to 4.6 per cent. By the early 1980s, in many inner cities, over a half of all young blacks were out-of-work (Roberts *et al.*, 1981).

Ethnic divisions are strengthened during work entry. Despite multiracial education, on leaving school black and Asian youth are not assimilated, but forced back into ethnic sub-cultures. West Indian and Asian youth face higher rates of unemployment even when, as is often the case, they leave school better qualified than local whites (Driver, 1980; Fuller, 1980; Roberts *et al.*, 1981). The superior performances of ethnic minority youth in many inner-city schools are not difficult to explain. Inner-city whites are a residue, many families with the means and motivation having departed. In contrast, the parents of present-day Asian and West Indian school-leavers are mostly first generation immigrants, and include many talented and ambitious people. Why else would they have crossed the oceans? Since settling in Britain they have been under-employed in unskilled jobs. They were told that they lacked relevant qualifications and skills, but many are determined that their children should succeed. They may not be able to provide the knowedgeable support available in middle-class homes, but Asian and West

Indian parents are no less keen that their children should do well. The pupils are encouraged to study and enrol in examination courses. Ethnic minority families want education to lead to qualifications that lead to jobs, and often display little interest in alternative, multi-cultural curricula (Stone, 1981).

Asian pupils are now equalling whites' performances. West Indian pupils still lag well behind the white population in general, but often out-perform whites from their own neighbourhoods and schools, which usually means entering the labour market with CSEs rather than completely unqualified. Ethnic minority youth leave better qualified and, on average, more ambitious than their white classmates (Gupta, 1977, Roberts *et al.*, 1981), but there are no grounds for describing their ambitions as unrealistic. The jobs to which most aspire are within the young people's abilities. They are not all demanding employment as brain surgeons and airline pilots. Most boys seek trades and training. The girls hope to work in offices, libraries, as receptionists and community workers. They are not demanding 'the best', but many are determined to avoid servile jobs. West Indian and Asian school-leavers are rarely content to accept 'anything'.

Ambitious West Indian and Asian youth are not necessarily keen to leave the neighbourhoods where they were reared. It is ordinarily taken for granted that aspiring whites from inner-city backgrounds hope to move to better areas. This is what 'getting on' is taken to mean. Ethnic minority families would appreciate better houses and surroundings. Nevertheless, given the prevailing social climate, many are ambivalent about leaving known people and places. Would they be accepted elsewhere? The wider society's deprived areas have become black youth's swinging places, their refuges and spiritual homes (Pryce, 1979). Many want better houses, education and employment prospects while they remain in Britain's Brixtons and Moss Sides. Does the wider society even understand this kind of ambition?

Asian and West Indian youth's qualifications and ambitions are rewarded with well-above-average rates of unemployment. Another difference is that minority youth have an obvious explanation for all their labour market difficulties—racial injustice. They are arrested by the same social class disadvantages faced by local whites. But no matter how strenuously and frequently sociologists argue their importance, social class divisions remain invisible. It is much easier to see skin pigmentation, and to many unemployed blacks and Asians, the explanation for their predicament is as clear as daylight—they are non-white citizens in a white society that is intent on holding them down, forcing them back. Black and Asian youth are less likely than whites to attribute their unemployment to 'bad luck', or accept it stoically as a fact of life, like the geographical terrain. Researchers have noted that black youth are among the most radical members of their entire generation (Rex and Tomlinson, 1979). Many, especially those influenced by Rastafarian doctrines (Garrison, 1979; Cashmore, 1979), are no longer seeking assimilation, or 'submersion'. They are turning inwards, drawing upon their own cultures, and looking to their own community organizations to help realize their ambitions.

Unemployment is not uniting black and white youth to address a common problem. It deepens racial divisions, and obstructs policies for racial equality. Ethnic minority youth's unemployment rates make the case for 'positive action', delivering better education, training and job opportunities. Blacks and Asians obtain their fair share of special measures (Stares, Imberg and McRobie, 1982), which would be reassuring if these opportunities always led to good jobs. The ethnic minorities are not seeking equality with their disadvantaged white neighbours. The latter's jobs and unemployment rates will not assuage the minorities' grievances. Why should they rest content with opportunities considered adequate only for the least privileged whites? Yet it would obviously be inflammatory to offer opportunities to inner-city blacks and Asians that were denied to their white neighbours. Positive discrimination and affirmative action in favour of women and ethnic minorities were originally proposed for context of full employment, economic expansion and growing opportunities for upward mobility.

Gender

The growth of female participation in the workforce has helped to generate pressures for equal pay and opportunities. At the beginning of the century only one in ten married women held paid employment. Women whose working lives were brief interludes before marriage may have conceded male breadwinners' prior claims in the competition for good jobs. Females' standards of living depended primarily on the occupations of their male heads of households—their fathers, then husbands. Employers saw no reason to waste training on female school-leavers who would attach greater importance to motherhood.

Today well over a half of married women are in employment. The majority of today's female school-leavers can expect to work outside their homes for the greater part of their adult lives. Even if their spouses are employed, women's earnings will be major, not marginal determinants of their families' living standards. Moreover, a third of today's marriages are expected to end in divorce or separation. Women can no longer rely upon marriage to deliver lifetime economic security. This is the background against which women won rights to equal pay for equal work, conferred by the 1970 Equal Pay Act, and to equal treatment in hiring and promotion in 1975.

It is common knowledge that these laws have yet to reshape the labour force. On average, women still earn a third less than men. Labour markets remain segmented. Female school-leavers are mainly recruited as office workers, shop assistants and factory operatives, when jobs are available. Management, jobs requiring scientific and technical qualifications, the prestigious professions and skilled trades remain male-dominated. Gender legislation has not changed employers' habits (Ashton and Maguire, 1980a). They still regard women as cheap and flexible, suitable jobs requiring little training but manual dexterity. Firms are still reluctant to invest in training young women.

Overt sex discrimination is disappearing from education. More girls than boys now enter 'O'-levels. Females are still under-represented in the universities, but their numbers are growing, to 37 per cent of undergraduates in 1982, and they are just as likely as males to enter some form of higher education. Colleges of Education recruit more women than men. Girls are still the less likely to succeed in maths and the physical sciences. A hidden curriculum which defines science as masculine and endorses teachers' acquiescence when clever girls fail to progress still operates. But schools and colleges are havens of equality compared with the labour market where their confinement to low-paid jobs perpetuates the idea that women's earnings are secondary and that husbands' careers should take precedence. While passing equal opportunity laws, governments have preserved social security regulations which treat married women as dependents.

Female school-leavers rarely allege unfair treatment (Allen and Smith, 1975). Individual acts of discrimination against women and ethnic minorities are equally difficult to prove. Until now, however, most girls have appeared satisfied with their inferior opportunities. Boys' and girls' vocational aspirations differ. Homes and schools separate the sexes' aspirations like the labour market divides their opportunities. Girls still see their futures primarily in terms of marriage. Their occupational horizons are short-term (Wilkins, 1955; Douvan and Adelson, 1966; Closs *et al.*, 1977). The sexes' aspirations are less divided than their actual occupations, but girls are still more likely than boys to abandon first choices and lower their sights when obstacles arise. An American study of unsuccessful medical school applicants found that women were less likely to reapply and more likely to abandon medicine for less prestigious careers (Weisman *et al.*, 1976).

If women's own aspirations were decisive there would be a trend towards equal representation throughout the occupational structure. Women doctors, managers, solicitors and motor mechanics would increase in number. But women's own wishes do not shape the entire labour market. Many employers still prefer to train males. Furthermore, male employees display little inclination to escape from their own enclaves and share women's work, unless the latter is upgraded, sometimes with shift premiums as in Lancashire textile mills. It is rare to encounter male school-leavers seeking jobs as typists, canteen assistants and switchboard operators. Men who perform women's work, whether by choice or necessity, may be regarded as 'odd'. Male nurses are considered unambitious and unattractive (Hesselbart, 1977). Males face greater difficulty in gaining acceptance in female occupations than women in formerly masculine jobs.

Between the wars, many studies of youth unemployment ignored girls; their lack of jobs and confinement to blind alleys were considered 'less of a problem'. It was believed that girls could withdraw into their homes without loss of face, occupy themselves with domestic duties and prepare for marriage. Women who did not marry and remained in employment were considered failures. Until World War I it was common for girls to be kept off school performing domestic duties during family emergencies, such as the illness of younger siblings. School Board officials sometimes turned a blind eye to these 'necessary' absences. After 1945, studies of school-leavers often concentrated upon boys. The latter's entry into employment was treated as a major status transition. Marriage and motherhood were regarded as the feminine equivalents. We do not know how earlier generations of girls felt about this role-typing, but recent female school-leavers have shared boys' worries about unemployment.

Youth unemployment has become equally prevalent among girls and boys. Competition from experienced married women and labour cutbacks in the light manufacturing industries that once recruited large numbers of female school-leavers have reduced girls' opportunities. During periods out-of-work, many girls still retreat into their homes, but few revel in the enforced domesticity (Donovan and Oddy, 1982). It is considered less acceptable for girls than boys to hang about in pubs, clubs, arcades and on the streets. Girls who are 'kept in' helping their mothers usually resent their confinement. They resent their isolation from youth scenes; their inability to dress in the latest fashions, attend discos and socialise with workmates (Roberts *et al.*, 1981).

There is anecdotal evidence, nothing more, of some unemployed girls drifting into the sex industries. Doctors and youth workers report instances of unemployed girls opting for early motherhood, thereby qualifying for more generous social security payments and independent housing, and establishing themselves in adult roles (Harold Francis, *Guardian* 30 December 1982). Will unemployment halt any trend towards equality and force women back into the domestic role? The latter has always concealed massive female unemployment. Some contemporary politicians regard domesticity for women as a solution to the wider society's unemployment problem. Many generations of teenage girls, confined to routine office and factory jobs, have seen marriage and motherhood as escape routes. Unemployment may be entrenching these preferences among some girls, but it seems unlikely that high levels of youth unemployment will provoke a general trend towards younger marriage and parenthood. In the full employment era, among young women, settling quickly in a chosen occupation was related to early marriage (Dex, 1982). Unemployment is more likely to impede than accelerate other aspects of social development. Moreover, male unemployment makes the traditional female role, supported by a male breadwinner, less accessible. In 1980 there were only three-fifths as many pregnancies among 15–19-year-olds as in 1971. There is further anecdotal evidence of some women, usually highly educated, refusing to 'retire' temporarily from employment for fear that they may never recover their jobs and occupational status. Males' and females' reactions to unemployment seem to vary by social class, like responses to educational and employment opportunities. These reactions may be helping to create an increasingly divided society. The number of households with both husbands and wives in well-paid jobs could increase, alongside a growth of families with neither partner in employment.

Government programmes to alleviate unemployment have catered equally for boys and girls, but are the schemes equally useful to the latter? Like jobs, training opportunities are still divided according to gender. Moreover, government measures appear designed to facilitate male careers in which, following initial training, individuals establish themselves in worthwhile jobs during their twenties. At this point in the life cycle, women tend to withdraw from the labour market. On what terms, if any, will young women who have recently retired to become parents be able to re-enter the workforce? Many will be unable to impress employers with their prior experience. Adult education and training rather than programmes aimed at teenagers, may be more effective in preventing women's disadvantages mounting while youth unemployment persists.

Cyclical and structural problem?

The rise of unemployment has been accompanied by a debate on the respective contributions of cyclical and structural factors. This controversy has more than academic significance. Prescriptions based on incorrect diagnoses will not deliver the intended cures.

Cyclical unemployment rises at troughs in the business cycle then disappears when the economy recovers. Structural unemployment is a term covering a variety of conditions which share in common only their intransigence in the face of general economic recovery. Simply 'throwing money at unemployment' is of no avail when the problem is structural. The decline of older industries such as textiles results in structural unemployment when firms shed workers, many of whom cannot be absorbed into expanding industries like banking and telecommunications, either because they lack relevant qualifications and skills or live in the wrong parts of the country.

All analysts agree that cyclical and structural factors have contributed during the rise of unemployment since the mid-1970s. The entire western economy entered a period of recession. National governments were reluctant to expand their economies for fear of pulling in imports, upsetting their trade balances, destroying the value of their currencies and stoking inflation, thereby building more serious problems for the future. The international community proved unable to act in concert, so the recession deepened, and accelerated structural changes including, in Britain, the decline of older industries with out-dated technologies. Where it exists, structural unemployment accentuates cyclical movements. With a permanent pool of job-seekers, employers can lay off workers in the knowledge that later recruitment will be no problem. This is one reason why high levels of unemployment and job mobility sometimes co-exist (White, n.d.).

Writers who allege that contemporary youth unemployment is structural accept that its growth has been accelerated by cyclical forces. Their argument is that straight-forward reflation, if and when it arrives, will not re-absorb all the young unemployed; that technological trends and the changing shape of the occupational structure will perpetuate young people's exclusion from jobs. Most job losses of the 1970s and early 1980s were caused by recession, not new technologies (Yates and Hall, 1982). Nevertheless, it is argued, reflation and new investment are now more likely to produce capital intensification, and higher output with labour forces of current or smaller sizes than increased employment (White, n.d.; Sawdon and Taylor, 1980).

Silicon chips could revolutionize work patterns in most offices and factories. Their applications are neither job- nor industry-specific. Robots can service assembly lines. Information can be stored and transmitted through microcircuits instead of by clerks. Rational decisions can be entrusted to computers instead of managers. The replacement of human workers by machines is not new. The internal combustion engine made horses and blacksmiths redundant. Mechanization and the container revolution have decimated dock workforces. It is possible to argue that forecasts of mass technological unemployment are not new and that the Luddites, then the later generation who believed that assembly line methods would cost factory jobs were proved mistaken. In the past new technologies have always led to new products, greater prosperity and more jobs than formerly. Optimists declare that today's new technologies will also increase employment once economic growth resumes, and provided we cease struggling to preserve old jobs and concentrate upon developing new products and services incorporating the latest techniques and components.

The problem with this strategy is that even if the diagnosis eventually proves correct, restoring full employment could take a long time, too long to benefit the 1970s', 1980s' and even the 1990s' school-leavers. Western economies seem unable to stimulate the investment and sustained growth to eradicate their current pools of unemployment. Predictions which link 'realistic' expectations of economic growth, maybe 2 per cent per year on average, with anticipated technological trends' implications for the demand for labour and the likely size of the workforce, lead to 'alarmist' forecasts of up to 6 million unemployed in Britain at the end of the century. In the long-term, new technologies may create additional employment, but we can be more confident that their short-term impact will be to destroy old jobs, and the gap before unemployment declines could span decades.

Insofar as new technology jobs are created, will 16-year-old school-leavers be able to perform them? If the jobs are within the young people's capacities, will they stand any chance in the competition for entry? If general unemployment remains high, what are young people's prospects, given employers' preference for older, experienced workers? Analyses which suggest that young people's problems are structural lead to proposals for structural remedies, and governments have grown increasingly receptive to these ideas. A series of special, temporary measures that could be dismantled when the recession ended, were governments' initial responses to rising youth unemployment. Current measures, including the YTS, are designed to last.

5

What Youth Unemployment Means

Rates and realities

The most frequently broadcast items of unemployment information are the rates and grand totals: 3,400,000 out of work, 14 per cent of the labour force, for example. These figures are the bread-and-butter of political debate. Their monthly publication is surrounded by media discussions of trends and prospects. Yet the statistics can mislead in several directions.

Variations in youth unemployment rates from month to month reveal little about trends over time. The rates are subject to wide seasonal fluctuations. They peak when Summer school-leavers sign on, then improve through every Autumn. The only meaningful comparisons are from year to year. Interpreters must also remember that these numbers and percentages exclude young people on special programmes. These individuals are not in employment; the majority are paid allowances, not wages. Yet the young people are not listed among the unemployed.

Further distortion occurs because some youth unemployment is unregistered. The numbers who fail to sign on vary considerably between different parts of the country. In some districts virtually all the young unemployed claim 'their rights', but in parts of London, in recent years, over 40 per cent have remained unregistered (Roberts et al., 1981). Some have 'not bothered', believing that their unemployment would be short-lived. Others have argued that 'the money isn't worth it'. Single 16-year-old school-leavers, living with their parents, are ineligible for Unemployment Benefit but can claim Supplementary Benefit, amounting to £15.80 in 1983. At age 18 the rate was £23.65, including £3.10 housing allowance. These sums are standard throughout the country. Where adult unemployment is high and wages low, parents expect young people to claim their entitlement. In contrast, many London families have argued that the amounts are insufficient compensation for the hassle and stigma of becoming claimants.

What snapshots conceal

An obvious way of translating percentages into human predicaments is to imagine that 20 per cent unemployment means that a fifth of all school-leavers in an area are sentenced to zero-prospects, but this rarely corresponds with the underlying reality. The published figures are snapshots, and cannot portray the flow into and out of the unemployed 'pool'. A European Economic Commission survey (1979) based on 9,118 interviews in nine member countries found that, between 1975 and 1978, 13 per cent of all workers had been unemployed for some period (19 per cent in the UK), and that 36 per cent had friends or close relatives who had suffered the experience. Unemployment rates have more than doubled since this enquiry. It is likely, therefore, that in any 3-year spell during the 1980s, over a third of Britain's workers will have spent some time unemployed. It seems certain that most people will now have relatives or close acquaints who have been victims. Over 3,000,000 out of work means that only a minority can feel completely secure. Even tenured academics have discovered that their positions are less secure than everyone believed.

Among the 3,000,000-plus who were unemployed in 1983, approximately 1,000,000 were 'long-term' cases, registered for over 12 months. Most spells out of work were much shorter, but many more than the individuals featured at single points in time passed through the pool during the year.

Public issue, personal solutions

With so much experience abroad, one might expect the unemployed to attract widespread sympathy. This does not necessarily follow. People who have been unemployed then regain work often expect others to do likewise. Unemployed teenagers soon grow tired of parents, uncles, aunts, neighbours, cousins and sometime friends explaining how *they* experienced difficulties, then found jobs. It is a constant irritation when the first question in every social encounter is, 'Are you still unemployed?' Are Britain's young unemployed regarded as deserving cases? Radio phone-ins and letters to the press still draw attention to the newspaper columns of vacancies, and how the boards seem full through Jobcentre windows. It frustrates the unemployed that so many jobs appear available when, on enquiry, they prove out of reach. Some newspapers carry pages of job adverts throughout periods of high unemployment, but the vacancies are exceeded many times over by the numbers seeking work. Young people find themselves ineligible for the majority of advertised jobs, even unskilled occupations, because they are too young or lack the experience demanded and offered by other applicants. Having been unemployed themselves does not mean that members of the wider public will sympathize when others suffer. Those who regain work often feel that they survived by searching, presenting themselves appropriately and accepting what was available. How many adults or even young people from other areas identify with the young unemployed in Brixton, Toxteth and Moss Side? If and when their own teenagers become unemployed, 'respectable' parents insist that their situation is very different from Britain's 'problem' cases and areas.

First reactions on becoming unemployed are usually to seek personal escapes. Like unemployed adults, jobless teenagers do not merge into a solidaristic army. They are divided by race, gender, education, family backgrounds and previous occupations. Many insist that they do not belong among 'that crowd', the dole queue regulars. It has been argued that the unemployed have not been mobilized as a political force because they are offered no ideologies linking their personal predicaments to political action (Scholzman and Verba, 1980). But another reason for preferring personal rather than collective solutions is that, for the majority, the former work. Most spells of joblessness end with individuals regaining employment. The majority of the population shares this experience. Hence the widespread expectation that individuals who find themselves without work, old and young, should 'get off their backsides' and struggle to obtain jobs, which is how most young people behave on becoming unemployed. Few display any interest in campaigns against youth unemployment. Of course, they argue that politicians should 'do something'. But the majority find it simpler and earn much greater respect by devising individual escapes than by uniting with their unemployed fellows. Clubs for the unemployed do not recruit huge memberships. The unemployed display little interest in concessionary admissions to cinemas and sports centres. They want to lose, not publicly proclaim, their unemployed status (Town, 1983).

Unemployment can be common while remaining a problem that many individuals face alone, or with support only from their immediate families and closest friends. Unemployment may be structurally inevitable while the victims are left feeling that *they* are failures, until they extricate themselves.

Sub-employment

When youth unemployment begins to rise, school-leavers' situations 'tighten'. Young people with good qualifications cease to receive several, and may have to accept sole job offers some time after leaving school. They may find it necessary to take stopgaps or settle for second-best jobs. Meanwhile, at the bottom of the educational procession, young people with poor or zero qualifications, who would have obtained unskilled jobs in times of full employment, face sub-employed early careers.

Chapter 3 explained that it has been customary for school-leavers who enter occupations offering no training to drift from job to job, reducing travelling costs whenever possible, and edging their earnings upwards. There are no rewards for inertia, so 'trivial' matters like quarrels with workmates, dislike of a foreman or just feeling 'pissed off' with the same routine can provoke departures.

Employers are rarely surprised when these young people quit. Firms recruiting school-leavers to unskilled jobs are seeking cheap, often temporary labour. The employers realize that they are offering neither the wages, conditions nor prospects to attract anyone they would wish to engage permanently. They do not hesitate to dismiss staff for poor work or timekeeping. An alternative is to make the employee's life at work miserable and provoke a 'voluntary' termination. Beginning workers have no legally enforceable job 'property rights', and trade union protection is rare in small businesses. For young, poorly qualified, unskilled workers, rising unemployment means that gaps between school-leaving and first jobs, then during subsequent job changes, become increasingly common, and lengthy. Instead of hopping directly from job to job with extended breaks at the young people's discretion, when they feel like 'holidays', their early work histories begin to consist of periods in work, interspersed with spells of unemployment. This 'sub-employed' career pattern occurs among unskilled adults who suffer repeatedly from the last in/first out custom, and who have no choice but to accept a succession of insecure jobs, many of which end involuntarily, while others prove not worth keeping (Norris, 1978). Sixty per cent of those who became unemployed in May 1980 obtained jobs within ten months, but 62 per cent of these left their new jobs within a further ten months, and a third became jobless again within a year of their initial spells ending (Labour Market Quarterly Report, MSC, February, 1983).

By the time youth unemployment reaches 15 per cent in districts where most young people leave school with modest qualifications to enter unskilled jobs, the majority of local school-leavers are experiencing spells out of work at some time or another (Roberts *et al.*, 1981). This is what 15 or 20 per cent youth unemployment in a locality usually means, rather than a fifth of all school-leavers being condemned to permanent idleness while the remainder obtain secure employment. Joblessness is spread around, and absorbed within sub-employed biographies.

In the late 1970s, with youth unemployment still at modest levels by the standards of the early 1980s (8 per cent in 1977) researchers began noting the very large proportions of school-leavers who were affected in certain areas. The school-leavers in the Youthaid (1979) enquiry were not worried about their forthcoming initiation into jobs. They were confident that they could handle any stresses in commencing employment but many were terrified by the prospect of unemployment, and not without cause, for 53 per cent had spells out of work during their first six months in the labour force. The consolation was that these jobless periods were usually brief, under 11 weeks on average. The majority of Pollock and Nicholson's (1981) 400 young people who left Scottish schools in 1976 encountered difficulty in finding work. Only 29 per cent were offered and accepted the first jobs they applied for, and 58 per cent had a taste of unemployment during their initial out-of-school year. However, only 4 per cent were continuously unemployed for over six months after leaving school. Unemployment was higher among young people than adults during the 1970s, but the young people's spells out of work were relatively brief (Daniel and Stilgoe, 1977). In 1977 the MSC observed that a third of all young people who became unemployed left the register within a month. The young people who risked and experienced unemployment most frequently were those who changed jobs most rapidly, namely, those entering unskilled occupations. They are the first group for whom rising unemployment makes a difference to the pattern of their early working lives, as opposed to just making the immediate transition from school to a chosen occupation more difficult. When youth unemployment recedes, early school-leavers in unskilled jobs will be the last group to be released from the effects.

Researchers and employment service staffs have noted how the young people at greatest risk often adapt to sub-employment with remarkable tolerance. Unemployment brings young people into more frequent contact with the employment services than formerly. They must register at Careers Offices or Jobcentres to claim social security. Visits do not normally lead to jobs, but nevertheless, most registrants express appreciation of career officers' efforts. The customers can understand employment staffs' difficulties when there are simply no jobs (Roberts *et al.*, 1981). In the Youthaid (1979) study, most jobs were found through other channels, but 72 per cent of the school-leavers rated their careers officers as helpful, and these officers emerged at the top of the list, named by 75 per cent of respondents, as the people to whom they would turn for future advice.

Few sub-employed young people blame the Careers Service or anyone else for their difficulties. They are apathetic rather than rebellious; as likely to blame themselves for their misfortunes as the wider society. In Rathkey's (1978) study of eighty-six unemployed 16–19-year-olds on Teeside, 75 per cent said they wished they had worked harder at school. But they realized full well that better qualifications would not guarantee good jobs. Unskilled youth experience the labour market as a lottery. Obtaining a job seems to depend mainly on luck—being in the right place at the right time, and 'hitting it off' with a prospective employer (Adams and Sawdon, 1978). Unemployed adults tend to be equally fatalistic. Jackson and Hanby (1982) studied 976 unemployed persons on government schemes in Scotland: 56 per cent did not support any political party, 73 per cent argued that a change of government would make little difference to the employment situation, and the majority felt that individuals on their own could do little to overcome their job-finding difficulties.

Sub-employment does not shatter career expectations when young people leave school seeking unskilled work. They do not anticipate settling in their initial occupations. In many of their neighbourhoods, 'breaks' between jobs have been normal throughout living memory (Phillips, 1973). Rising unemployment simply lengthens these episodes, and increases their frequency. The threat of unemployment does not always inhibit young unskilled workers' job changing. Maintaining self-respect and status in the eyes of peers sometimes requires young people to quit, not cling to 'trash jobs'. When unemployed, they are not always willing to accept any job. Some decline to be submitted for vacancies to which the employment services draw their attention. Even the young unemployed maintain certain standards, like expecting to be paid for working. They hesitate before considering jobs where the wages, less travelling and other costs, barely exceed social security entitlements.

When there are insufficient jobs to accommodate all would-be workers, unemployment for some is inevitable, but the victims may still feel in control of their destinies. How long individuals remain unemployed can depend on the standards they preserve. With local unemployment approaching 30 per cent, jobless youth in urban areas do not face zero prospects. There are always jobs being vacated to search and apply for, though not necessarily through the statutory services. Needless to say, individuals' standards can change during jobless episodes. When it seems unlikely that something preferable will turn up, most young people will consider 'anything', even places on government schemes when they realize full well that these opportunities are likely to lead back to unemployment. Special measures, to date, have not led young people to permanent jobs or 'up' the labour market into skilled employment, but have kept sub-employed youth afloat, in circulation. They have helped to preserve work habits and motivation, and reduced the numbers who would otherwise have descended into long-term unemployment.

Long-term youth unemployment

It is impossible to draw a precise boundary at three, six or twelve months, separating short- from long-term unemployment. Nevertheless, there is a qualitative difference. After a time, which can vary from person to person, individuals cease thinking of themselves as 'between jobs' or 'looking for work', and grow resigned to having joined 'the unemployed'. When this occurs, job seeking becomes nominal, if it continues. Fruitless job hunting is soul-destroying. Rejections are painful, more so than joblessness itself. Individuals become trapped in the situation where their own histories of joblessness are additional handicaps in the search for work. At age 19 or 20, with no substantial work experience, young adults who have grown accustomed to idleness are less attractive to employers than 'nice fresh school-leavers'. The over-18s are rarely willing to work for youth wages, while self-interested employers can hardly be expected to recruit the longer-term unemployed when the jobs attract experienced adults. This is how the long-term young unemployed become a 'hard-core'. Employment services staffs sometimes confess that their situations are hopeless.

While unemployment in local youth labour markets remains at 'modest' levels, beneath 25 per cent, only small minorities of 'young people with problems' descend into hardcore predicaments (Roberts, Noble and Duggan, 1982a, 1982b). They may be poor interviewees, repeatedly rejected applicants, suffer acute shyness, offend employers with 'way out' manners or appearances, or possess serious criminal records. The chronic job changers of earlier years find, in tighter labour markets, that job offers soon disappear (Baxter, 1975). After two or even just one very short-lived job, terminated by the young person for no pressing reason or by a dissatisfied employer, an individual can discover that other firms simply 'don't want to know'.

Beyond some level, which as yet cannot be precisely defined, youth unemployment ceases to be concentrated in 'deprived areas' where the majority of young people leave school with modest qualifications, if any, hoping for unskilled jobs. School-leavers who expected stable employment in progressive careers, from families who believed that unemployment was a newspaper problem that happened to other people, find their difficulties extending beyond delays after school-leaving, waiting until acceptable jobs are available. These young people and parents often find unemployment impossible to accept. Young people who have been taught at home that the unemployed are 'bone-idle and useless, unable to cope even with simple tasks like washing dishes', dread the prospect. Girls from middle-class homes do not regard impoverished motherhood as an escape:

> I won't be able to marry and have children. I won't be able to save for a house, to pay for clothes and other everyday accessories. It would be worse if the person I married was also unemployed. We just couldn't carry on with life.

Some young people and parents in middle-class districts who find their qualifications earning near-zero prospects can be relied upon to make their annoyance known to the press, local councillors, MPs, teachers and careers officers. They demand real opportunities, not palliatives. Some return to education. In 1982–3 the MSC under-spent by 20 per cent. mainly because young people began staying at school instead of flocking into the Youth Opportunities Programme (see Chapter 6) in their anticipated numbers.

By the time youth unemployment is causing anxiety among young people and parents who believed that their qualifications and contacts made them safe, long-term unemployment is spreading rapidly in many districts where sub-employment had already become normal. As local rates rise above 30 per cent, unemployment cannot be absorbed in transitory episodes, and young people without special problems or handicaps, who would have obtained and retained jobs without difficulty had any been available, descend into the hardcore. In inner Liverpool in 1980, over a third of school-leavers were heading for long-term unemployment (Roberts *et al.*, 1982). As joblessness continued to rise in the early 1980s, this scene must have been repeated in blackspots throughout the country. Government schemes were unable to stem the tide. Young people 'benefited' from special measures then became long-term unemployed.

The experience of unemployment

No-one disagrees that young people and, indeed, society in general would benefit if youth unemployment was eradicated, but there is a division of opinion on the extent and ways in which young people are damaged and the 'social fabric' weakened while youth unemployment persists. The gut reaction of many writers and researchers has been indignation and horror. Unemployment research has always been prompted by political in addition to academic motives. The 1930s' studies which have recently been rescued from dusty library shelves, were intended and succeeded in helping to create the political climate in which mass unemployment was condemned as intolerable, and politicians of all parties vowed that it would never return. Inter-war researchers explained that, for most people, jobs are more than sources of income. They confer social status, positions in the community, and give individuals a sense of identity. The unemployed suffer financial hardship, and more besides. They lose social esteem. Personalities can disintegrate when stripped of their occupational supports.

Marie Jahoda (1979, 1982), a survivor from the earlier generation of researchers, has reviewed 112 of the inter-war studies, re-emphasized the personal demoralization and social decay that spread during the Great Depression, and has argued from a smaller number of recent enquiries that the effects of unemployment today are basically unchanged. Other writers have echoed this position, insisting that poverty, stigma, shame and social isolation descend as harshly as ever (Sinfield, 1981; Marsden, 1982). Hill's (1978) interviews with unemployed adults offer evidence of responses to job loss, then prolonged unemployment passing through the same stages that were identified in the 1930s.

Shock is a common initial reaction. Individuals who are thrown out of work find it hard to believe that unemployment is happening to them. The situation feels unreal. Sometimes a holiday atmosphere develops. Workers declared redundant assure one another that *they* will not remain unemployed for long, given their experience, skills and contacts. They begin applying for jobs optimistically, sometimes enthusiastically. They are not 'unemployed' but 'looking for work'. Locating and applying for jobs can be treated as an occupation. The second stage is one of frustration and increasing pessimism as enquiries are unanswered and applications rejected. Individuals can find it difficult to understand their lack of success. They begin to query their job search tactics. Eventually they question their own worth. Self-confidence ebbs. During the third and final phase fatalism and apathy descend. Individuals begin adjusting to life without work. Daily routines geared to employment collapse. Some individuals behave aggressively towards other members of their families as they attempt to protect their disappearing status. Others simply withdraw. The long-term unemployed become isolated from former friends by poverty and the stigma of joblessness. The everyday, getting-acquainted question, 'What do you do?' is ordinarily taken to mean 'What work?' Stripped of employment, individuals lack credible identities. Social intercourse then becomes painful.

Some researchers claim that unemployment actually kills. A wide variety of physical illnesses are associated with unemployment. Stern (1982) has reminded us that correlations do not always indicate causation, that there are cases of physical fitness improving when individuals leave unhealthy jobs, and of mental health recovering when people escape from the stresses of work. In general, however, the evidence is clear; unemployment is harmful.

Could leisure interests serve as substitutes for jobs? This seems doubtful (Kelvin, 1981). Leisure activities do not generate income. Moreover, while they can fill time, leisure pursuits, being voluntary, cannot impose a structure on days, weeks and months. Insofar as they are practised for intrinsic personal rewards rather than for their value to others, leisure interests cannot become bases for socially esteemed identities. There are examples from the 1980s of claimants taking care to avoid neighbours when signing on; they have no wish to advertise their inability to regain work. There are also examples of out-of-work men who rate signing on as a highlight of their week; an opportunity to go out and meet people (Morley-Bunker, 1982). It is far more difficult to find evidence of the unemployed becoming a new leisure class. The Association of Recreation Managers (1981) has found scant evidence of successful programmes for the unemployed. This is not only because the unemployed are a fluid population from whom no long-term commitment can be expected, and because reduced charges may still be too high while even free access will not attract the bored and isolated (Town, 1983). Free admissions to sports halls are simply no solution to the problems of families struggling on low incomes. Opportunities to play are no answer when people want jobs.

From their research among young people in employment, unemployed and at school in a Scottish city, Hendry, Raymond and Stewart (1983) argue that work and leisure are 'a package'. Leisure loses its meaning when individuals have no jobs. The unemployed have expanses of spare time rather than leisure. Hence the inability of leisure services to solve the unemployed's problems. Hendry *et al.* (1983) argue that their inability to implement the work–leisure package frustrates and disorients school-leavers, and interferes with the process of growing up.

The black economy is another red herring. Rumours abound of claimants working unofficially, but in practice the individuals best placed to operate the black economy are skilled adults who can repair houses, cars and suchlike. Young people in employment are more likely to hold part-time jobs than the young unemployed (Roberts *et al.*, 1981). The latter often express keen interest in 'a bit on the side'. Unfortunately for them, in high unemployment areas there is intense competition for casual work and, as in the formal economy, young people tend to lose out. Careers advisors debate the wisdom of equipping school-leavers with 'survival packages' and encouraging them to exploit opportunities in the black economy (Watts, 1978, 1981; Hearn, 1981). The problem is that the search for 'sidelines' can be as frustrating as the competition for real jobs, and when obtained, casual work is slave labour par excellence— chronically insecure and low paid. There are very few young people who treat either criminal enterprise or casual work as genuine alternatives to proper jobs. Some people may find the black economy a source of satisfying work and an outlet for entrepreneurial talents. For young people, however, it is rarely more than a temporary buffer and survival mechanism (Henry, 1982).

Is youth unemployment especially damaging?

Some writers claim that unemployment is always distressing, and that *youth* unemployment is especially damaging, because adolescence is the stage at which individuals must establish adult identities. Young people are stripped of childhood statuses and the security they offered. Adolescents are expected to grow up, leave school and become independent of their families. They need to redefine their relationships with parents. Independence is often practised during leisure, but with the status in addition to the income supplied by employment. Schools have responded to unemployment by strengthening their attempts at vocational preparation rather than by preparing young people to live without work. No alternative life styles are offered. Unemployment is uniformly defined as a problem by teachers, politicians and the media. As a result, jobless teenagers lack relevant aims and motivations. Their mental health deteriorates during spells out of work, (Jackson and Stafford, 1980). Compared with young people in jobs, the young unemployed are less satisfied with life, have lower self-esteem, suffer greater depression and anxiety, and have lower social and family adjustment scores, though good family relationships, where they exist and are maintained, appear capable of alleviating other problems (Donovan and Oddy, 1982). It has been argued that leaving young people without jobs or adequate substitutes for prolonged periods could endanger not only the individuals' welfare but the wider society. Will the young unemployed learn to live without jobs? Will they settle in daily routines that subsequently prove impossible to break? Will youth unemployment lead to a decomposition of labour power; a permanent loss of the ability and will to work?

According to Eggleston (1979):

> Unless a balanced, satisfying vocational identity can be achieved, then life for the individual is likely to be at best incomplete or compartmentalised; at worst, frustrating, enervating and incompatible.... At no stage in life are these issues of identity more important than in the formative years of adolescence when predominantly childhood roles and identities have to be replaced or augmented by those of adult life.

Ridley (1981) argues that:

> ... though the adult unemployed may experience the greater financial hardship, it is for the juvenile that the experience is likely to be most traumatic, because he is at the most vulnerable age emotionally.

Economic and technological changes are de-structuring work entry. Society's institutions, schools and employment, no longer interlock, and it is argued that young people are being left to bear the costs. In the past the compensations for educational failure and limited career prospects were early opportunities to earn adult wages in semi- and unskilled jobs. We have been warned that young people who feel rejected by society will reject that society. The 1981 street riots stirred fears of the young unemployed threatening social order. The costs of youth unemployment are said to include unprecedented crime and policing problems, alienated and embittered young adults, available for mobilization by extremist political movements.

However, there is a contrary argument; that unemployment is far less devastating for young people than adults, and that the former are often able to cope with no long-term damage to themselves or the wider society. Needless to say, arguing that young people can tolerate un-employment is not the same as condoning the need for them to do so.

There are several strands to the argument that 'young people can cope'. First, it is argued that unemployment today cannot be 'basically the same' experience as in the 1930s. Surely the experience must vary with the social context (Pahl, 1982). The majority of the young unem-ployed in the 1980s are not from families enduring the same material hardship that spread between the wars. Today's young people have been born and bred in a welfare state, and despite repeated press campaigns against 'scroungers', many treat its support as a right, not charity. Unlike in the 1930s, unemployed young people's families do not have to prove their poverty before relief is offered. Moreover, since the war it has become more common and acceptable for 16–19-year-olds to be supported by parents, usually while continuing their education. Even in working-class areas, it is no longer taken for granted that young people will be earning at 16. Young adult independence can be achieved without wage-earning status.

Second, it is pointed out that school-leavers have no occupational identities to shatter, and that their personalities cannot be assaulted in quite the same way as life-long steelworkers and dockers. Furthermore, school-leavers have the better grounds for hope. They can realistically expect their prospects to improve, unlike the redundant middle-aged, many of whom are sentenced to *de facto* early retirement. Irrespective of Britain's economic fortunes, time improves school-leavers' prospects. They have only to grow older to overcome employers' prejudice against teenagers, and to compete for jobs involving shift work, driving and other skills. Follow-up studies have shown that the children of the Great Depression and more recent school-leavers who drifted into intermittent employment recovered from the experience (Elder, 1974; Cherry, 1976).

Third, it is pointed out that a great deal of youth unemployment is splintered into short episodes, and that the victims are concentrated in areas where early careers moving between unskilled jobs, sometimes separated by 'breaks' are customary (Phillips, 1973). Additional unemployment can be absorbed without shattering these young people's expectations.

Fourth, attention is drawn to how the deprivations of unemployment are always relative to the rewards that employment confers. One recent study suggests that sub-employed youth are more damaged by disagreeable, boring, alienating and sometimes dangerous jobs, than by their spells out of work (Pahl and Wallace, 1980). Few young people claim to enjoy unemployment; but the main problems they experience are not so much stigmatization, as boredom and poverty, which often persist when they are working. The jobs they sample are mostly boring and low paid. Some reserve their most vociferous criticisms for the jobs and schemes they have experienced or been invited to consider. A common view is that neither work nor unemployment are tolerable for long unbroken periods. Sub-employment then becomes a preferred way of life. The young people remain afloat, in circulation, above the hardcore, but settle for working intermittently. Many make it clear that they have no intention of 'selling out' and settling in 'trash jobs'. The EEC inquiry (1979) referred to earlier noted that unemployed 15–24-year-olds were more 'intransigent' than adults; less willing to learn new skills or consider moving to different areas. Rather than developing occupational identities, some young people strive to protect, and refuse to sell their 'real' selves for 'slave wages' in 'shit jobs'.

Fifth, it is argued that the trend over time where youth unemployment persists, is not for discontents to fester and eventually explode, but for young people to become accustomed, adapt and cope with the predicament. In regions where unemployment persisted through the 1950s and 60s, survival skills have passed down the generations. Children learn from adults how to survive on low incomes. Parents teach young people how to claim 'their rights'. Elsewhere, young people have been generating these skills within their peer groups. Unemployment impoverishes adults' leisure and reduces social intercourse (Parry, 1980; Bunker, Dewberry and Kelvin, 1983). In contrast, among the under-21s unemployment increases the amounts of time that friends spend together (Morley-Bunker, 1982). The billiard hall culture has been revived, though nowadays the video arcade is a more common alternative to the streets for young people with time on their hands. During spells out of work, young people scale down rather than abandon normal leisure spending, and appear to make this adjustment without profound psychological repercussions (Willis, 1979). Some writers claim that the young sub-employed are pace-setters, pioneers of flexible life styles who are claiming their 'right to useful unemployment' (Illich, 1978), learning to enjoy 'occupational marginality' (Rousselet, 1979), and adapting to discontinuous patterns of employment that more and more people will be obliged to accept (Willis, 1979).

The social context

Have we under-estimated the victims' tolerance and the wider social system's ability to absorb unemployment? It used to be said that the country would never again tolerate 1,000,000, then 2,000,000, then 3,000,000 out of work. These levels are now being endured. Some American commentators have been asking whether, despite the swollen levels, Europe's youth unemployment amounts to 'a problem' (Gordon, 1979).

In the USA throughout the 1960s unemployment among 16–21-year-olds who had left full-time education stubbornly refused to fall beneath

20 per cent. In many inner cities the rates rose and remain above 50 per cent. These levels have been described as 'social dynamite' (Conant, 1965). America's schools, like Britain's have been accused of failing to provide early leavers with marketable skills. Remedial projects have been launched to equip chronically unemployed youth with elementary skills and stable work habits (Rist, 1982). American industry has been criticized for failing to provide on-the-job training for the nation's youth. The USA does not share Europe's apprenticeship tradition—the practice of commencing vocational training at young ages within surrogate-parent relationships. American employers prefer to train older recruits who are considered safer bets—more eager to learn, mature and responsible, and rather than training which lasts several years, US firms normally provide incremental modules through which individuals can gradually add to their skills as their careers progress. These arrangements confine out-of-school teenagers to the margins of the labour market, which is one reason why the majority of US youth remain in education to graduate high school, and why 50 per cent proceed to college. The 16–21 year-olds of whom 20 per cent are unemployed are not the majority of their age groups. Needless to say, once it becomes normal for able and ambitious young people to remain in education, the disadvantages of those who leave escalate. They are the tail end of failures who employers seek to avoid rather than recruit.

Americans are not complacent about their high school drop outs who sink into long-term unemployment, especially in the inner cities where dropping out is normal, not deviant. But many commentators take a different view of the predicaments of young Americans who drift in and out of education, and in and out of jobs while they work their way towards, then through college. Milling around while deferring commitment to any lifetime career, surviving on casual employment in garages and for Macdonalds, are accepted parts of the American youth scene. Young people often appreciate the variety while drifting in and out of unskilled jobs, living through periods of unemployment with support from families, savings and the welfare state (Gaskell and Lazerson, 1980). This experience is considered educative for young people with the ability to survive, the qualifications to opt back in, and opportunities to settle in progressive careers during their twenties.

Observers who have queried whether Europe's youth unemployment is a problem have noted the extent to which joblessness is absorbed in sub-employed early careers, and have offered America's experience as proof that intermittent employment need not leave permanent scars and, indeed, may be preferred to continuous employment or education. Has Europe been reacting to rising unemployment with attitudes bred in an earlier era which are now outdated? Europe has a tradition of apprentice training. Our ideal path to adulthood emancipates young people from parents while shielding them in pastoral relationships with teachers, then trainee status at work, before releasing them into steady jobs or progressive careers. Drifting around violates deeply ingrained ideas about how youth should be spent—preferably getting ahead, preparing seriously for lifetime careers by amassing credentials, completing recognized training programmes or, at least, building stable employment histories. Should we be applauding young people's survival skills instead of deploring a youth unemployment problem?

American standards are probably as misleading as attitudes formed during the Great Depression when appraising youth unemployment in contemporary Europe. The majority of out-of-work teenagers in Britain have no opportunity to drift back into the educational mainstream. Nor can they expect training opportunities at later stages as rewards for remaining afloat during their initial out-of-school years. The evidence and debate about whether young people are exceptionally damaged or better able to cope with unemployment is demonstrating that the experience varies immensely with the context, and that there is no single 'youth reaction'. The effects depend upon the type of unemployment— transitory or long-term. It is only the former that is said to be tolerable. No-one claims that long-term joblessness is anything but depressing and damaging. Reactions to unemployment also depend upon which young people are affected. Unqualified school-leavers from unskilled working-class homes, and young people with impressive credentials and aspiring parents do not respond in identical ways when offered (or denied) identical opportunities. Boys' peer groups are more resilient than girls'. The former are the more skilled in colonizing streets and other environments to enjoy each other's company. Rather than finding it 'less of a problem', girls may be the more injured by unemployment. Unemployed ethnic minority youth appear less likely than native-born whites to accept their bad luck, and more likely to regard themselves as victims of an unjust society.

Hendry *et al.* (1983) distinguished three experiences of unemployment among their Scottish sample. Some welcomed the 'vacational' experience of a break or holiday. Others treated unemployment as 'a vocation' by making an occupation out of job hunting or, if females, domestic work. However, the most common experience of unemployment was 'an ordeal'. Even the coping unemployed are living with a problem. The young people's ability to adapt will not necessarily justify the wider society leaving them to do so. But policies to deal with youth unemployment must take account of young people's own survival skills. The young unemployed are not so uniformly demoralized as to gratefully seize any alternatives—any schemes or jobs, however pointless the work, and however low-paid. The wider society's solutions to youth unemployment now feature among some school-leavers' problems.

6

Government Responses

Special measures

We, the British, are considered a pragmatic people. We take pride in our serendipity, the happy knack of muddling through and achieving desired outcomes without even defining our goals, let alone carefully selecting the means. We are suspicious of intellectually elegant solutions. We would have surprised ourselves and the rest of the world had we formulated comprehensive plans for the transition into employment, relating the numbers of young people we know will complete education each year until the mid-1990s to the likely shape of the occupational structure, then built bridges linking the two.

Governments cannot be accused of inactivity in the face of rising youth unemployment. Since 1975 school-leavers have been assailed with schemes and programmes offering education, training, work preparation and work experience. There is no reason to doubt politicians' sincerity in wanting to do something for school-leavers, but each new initiative has been an implied confession of its predecessor's limitations. The rapid birth and obsolescence of titles indicates the speed at which programmes have lost credibility, and has invited suspicion that their real political role is cosmetic—to reduce embarrassing unemployment totals without actually creating more employment, and to disguise the fact that the economy cannot occupy young people.

School-leavers have been offered new opportunities, but have their prospects improved? Or are their problems simply deferred? School-leaver unemployment was the main transition problem of the late-1970s. Governments pledged themselves to Easter then Christmas guarantees—a job or scheme offer for every school-leaver. The problems of the mid-1980s are different. Most 16- and 17-year-olds are now in education or training. Only a minority obtain ordinary jobs. Some remain unemployed. But the main problem is no longer stemming joblessness among

16-year-olds. It is the transition at 17 plus, following extended education or initial training that worries young people, parents, their advisors and politicians.

Britain is just one of many western countries where school-leavers now face labour, education and training markets that are poorer than ever in real jobs, but richer than ever in schemes and courses. The young people's problem is that few of these opportunities are reliable roads to adult employment. Continuing in education is a sound bet for teenagers who expect to obtain good 'A'-levels and proceed to university, but are young people who complete full-time education at 17 or 18 enhancing their prospects by staying on? Traditional apprenticeships remain popular. Can young people have comparable confidence in the new training schemes leading to skilled status, or any deferred rewards?

Previous chapters explained how, throughout the post-war decades, most young people travelled along clear roads towards adult employment, developed realistic aspirations then made smooth transitions. These transitions are now prolonged for the majority and apparently never-ending for some. Whether some school-leavers' opportunities will ever lead to secure jobs consistent with their abilities, qualifications and aspirations is uncertain. Young people are now thrust into a limbo of waiting rooms—low-paid temporary jobs, courses, and schemes that offer experience of work tasks in work environments but withhold 'real worker' identity and status (Watts, 1980). The uncertainties are real, not products of young people's ignorance.

There were hopes, when unemployment forced governments to propose remedies and 'do something' about school-leavers' plights, that the reconstruction would tackle not only teenage joblessness but longer-standing problems. Some clear roads which transported earlier generations of school-leavers were too narrow while others, particularly those involving no training or further education, were too wide to prepare the adult workforce that an advanced industrial economy requires. Despite a half-century of educational reform, opportunities remained heavily dependent on social origins. Moreover, young people were forced to make crucial decisions, or had such decisions made for them during early adolescence, before they were aware of the long-term implications, or even of their own talents and interests. It was hoped that youth unemployment could be relieved in ways that would simultaneously address these older issues: that the transition could become gradual, enabling individuals to test their inclinations and abilities in different courses and work environments before taking irreversible decisions, and that a better match might be achieved between young people's qualifications and skills, and future job requirements. By 1983, when the YTS was launched, much of this optimism had evaporated. There was little confidence outside MSC brochures that the initiative would amount to progress compared with the prospects that awaited the 1950s' and 1960s' school-leavers. Unemployment had risen steeply among 18–25-year-olds. Earlier special measures had left many young adults floundering on the margins of the workforce.

Job Creation Projects

The first government initiatives were introduced as temporary measures to address, it was hoped, a short-lived youth unemployment problem. Subsidies were offered to employers who hired longer-term unemployed young people and in October 1975 the Job Creation Projects (JCPs), the direct ancestors of the YTS were launched. JCPs were government-funded, but were usually proposed and managed by voluntary agencies and local authorities to perform work of value to the wider community. There has always been plentiful scope for such work, but projects could only be approved if they were not competing with commercial enterprises otherwise industry would have objected, and if the work would not normally have been undertaken by mainstream public services otherwise the trade unions would have been opposed. Within these limits, particularly when speed is the essence, it is not always easy to create *useful* jobs, which is why newspaper stories soon appeared ridiculing schemes where, for example, young people cleared graffiti that always reappeared the next day.

In his study of projects in Wales, Jenkins (1983) noted how the most useful schemes always seemed to be pressing the limits of the eligibility rules. When a genuine community demand exists, work is usually adopted by commercial or mainstream public services. Nevertheless, a great deal of useful work was undertaken and continues on schemes that have replaced JCPs. All the relevant studies report that the community at large derives real benefits (Jenkins, 1983; Duffy, 1982). Otherwise unemployed persons have improved country parks, urban playgrounds, coastal areas, footpaths, derelict sites, community halls and museums. They have insulated and performed other repairs to elderly and disabled citizens' homes, and strengthened the voluntary social services. The main problem with community schemes is not that the work is pointless, but that creating special projects for the unemployed is often an inefficient way of accomplishing it. Environmental improvements could sometimes be achieved more quickly and cheaply using capital rather than labour-intensive methods. Some of the work would be performed more efficiently by skilled and experienced workers rather than individuals with no alternative to unemployment other than temporary low-paid posts (Jenkins, 1983).

When the JCPs were launched, young people were defined as a priority group, but job creation was also intended to assist unemployed adults. School-leavers and adults worked side by side on many early projects. However, it soon became apparent that different age groups had different vocational needs and abilities, and in 1976 a Work Experience Programme (WEP) for 16–18-year-olds was separated from the JCPs that continued to cater for older persons. Work experience placed less emphasis on community benefits, and more upon training in basic work skills and habits, thereby enhancing young people's employability.

The JCPs and WEP were not abysmal failures. They were not abandoned but absorbed into subsequent special measures. Job creation for adults continued under the Special Temporary Employment Programme, which became the Community Enterprise Programme, then the Community Programme in 1982. As explained below, WEP was absorbed into the larger YOP. The initial measures did not fail to achieve their architects' hopes. The problem was that their aims were outstripped by the persistent growth of unemployment. With joblessness spreading, subsidies were unable to prevent the numbers of young and adult long-term unemployed growing, and it proved impossible to generate projects apace.

The Youth Opportunities Programme

In 1978 the YOP was launched by the MSC to absorb and add to existing provisions for the young unemployed. There were two main branches in the programme. The larger and better-known—WEP—catered for 450,000 young people in 1981–82. Four types of work experience were offered. Project-based and community service schemes absorbed WEP (Brelsford, Rix and Smith, 1981). Other schemes were based in workshops run by local authorities, training boards, firms and by the MSC itself (Dungate, 1982). However, the most common form of work experience was on employers' premises. YOP expanded provisions for the young unemployed mainly by allowing private industry and mainstream public services to participate.

Employers were encouraged to accept unemployed young people, usually for six months but sometimes longer, and provide 'experience' in work environments. There was no cost to employers. Trainees' allowances, £25 by 1982, plus overheads, were reimbursed by the MSC. Work experience trainees were usually based in industry, but in many instances college attendance was built into their training. Employers and further education colleges were encouraged to co-operate, MSC funds were offered at a time of cutbacks in other areas of educational spending, and the Commission even provided some educational packages for colleges to implement, in Social and Life Skills for example.

Work Preparation was YOP's second branch (Hemborough et al. 1982). Courses based in schools, colleges or workshops lasted up to 10 weeks and handled 100,000 trainees in 1981-2. Preparatory courses were used prior to work experience or job applications when young people's work attitudes or habits needed sharpening following prolonged unemployment, intermittent school attendance, or when individuals lacked the confidence to face unsheltered work environments. These courses were also used as a screening process to assess trainees' suitability for different types of eventual employment.

The entire programme was introduced rapidly and successfully amidst the 'moral panic' that mounting youth unemployment provoked among politicians and in the press (Rees and Atkinson, 1982). There were fears that demoralized youth would turn anti-social, and alarm at the nation's human resources being wasted with long-term implications if the young unemployed lost the ability and will to work. The MSC was successful in selling YOP to industry. Letters, phone calls and personal visits, backed by television and newspaper adverts persuaded firms that the young unemployed were deserving cases, and that industry's self interests would be served by offering work experience as an alternative to idleness. In April 1979, during YOP's first full year, there were only 1,600 cases across the entire country where the Easter undertaking, an offer of a YOP place to every unemployed school-leaver, remained unfulfilled (Manpower Services Commission, 1979). The programme was sold to young people with more television and newspaper adverts, posters in schools and careers offices, and radio roadshows. In some areas, school-leavers were initially resistant to being sent on schemes and thereby withdrawn from the competition for real jobs. But the realization soon dawned that YOP was becoming a necessary prelude to a real job in most parts of Britain. Before long the acronym had been assimilated into the youth culture and school-leavers anticipated schemes as a normal stage in their careers (Duffy, 1982).

All YOP participants, on Work Preparation and all forms of Work Experience always received the same standard allowance, unlike the former practice on JCPs of paying the local rate for the job. The programme was always voluntary. Employers who offered work experience, and the young people were volunteers. There was no conscription.

Young people could decline places without losing social security entitlement. Employers have never favoured compulsion. They would be reluctant to volunteer as custodians of unwilling trainees. Department of Employment proposals in 1981 to reduce trainees' allowances from £25 to £15, and to end 16-year-olds' right to Supplementary Benefit were withdrawn in the face of concerted opposition from the MSC, trade unions and employers (Manpower Services Commission, 1982)

The Training for Skills Programme

Outside YOP the MSC had two additional measures for tackling youth unemployment. Grants were awarded under the Training for Skills Programme to help maintain apprentice training during the recession. All possible efforts were made to enable young people to continue training when firms ceased trading, or found it necessary to declare apprentices redundant. Grants were also made to help firms maintain normal apprentice intakes despite short-term financial difficulties. During 1981–2 35,000 young people were assisted through this scheme.

Community Industry

Community Industry (CI) pre-dates all other special measures. It began in 1972 before youth unemployment became a national problem (Murray, 1978). This scheme, which is still in operation, performs work of value to the wider community, like the JCPs, but was designed for young people who could not obtain or settle in employment, not because there were no jobs, but because the individuals were unable to cope, failed to adjust, or were repeatedly dismissed for unsatisfactory work, conduct or attendance. Recruits to CI are mostly unqualified school-leavers who suffer additional disadvantages such as broken homes, disturbed childhoods and/or criminal records, but scheme organizers usually attempt to recruit 'judicious mixtures'. The projects would collapse if all trainees were extreme problem cases. As general youth unemployment rose during the 1970s, organizers became able to select recruits. In 1982 there were only 7,000 CI places in the entire country. CI placements normally last 12 months, and trainees are paid wages rather than allowances, so tax and National Insurance are deducted. In 1982, in the provinces, 16-year-olds received £29.70, and 18-year-olds were paid £37.80—significantly in excess of the remuneration on other young people's schemes.

Another attraction is that CI often provides interesting work. The schemes are permanent and, during their history, sometimes by trial and error, have discovered many absorbing and worthwhile jobs. Some projects have developed into commercially viable co-operative ventures. However, most trainees are still 'young people with problems'. A follow-up study of 1978 entrants (Shanks, 1982) found that most left for unskilled work or unemployment, but nearly all felt that the CI experience had been worthwhile. CI was originally devised and is still administered by the National Association of Youth Clubs, but is overseen and financed through the MSC.

Verdicts on the Youth Opportunities Programme

Evaluations of YOP varied with the assessors' standards. The facts were never in dispute so much as the yardsticks. All observers agreed that the programme was restructuring the entire process of work entry. Instead of a transition from school to work, the normal sequence became from school to schemes to jobs, with spells of unemployment complicating and sometimes preventing progress.

In 1979 the Institute of Careers Officers welcomed YOP as the most important post-1945 development in training for young people. This programme and its successors have certainly altered the balance in the Careers Service's own work. Generic careers work used to be performed in secondary schools, preparing young people for work entry. Once school-leavers were assisted into their first jobs, the majority lost contact with the Careers Service. Since the rise of youth unemployment, additional careers officers have been appointed to assist young people into then out of special measures. Initially these posts were treated as special and temporary, but they are proving permanent, rather than peripheral, and assisting out-of-school youth has become mainstream careers work.

YOP was designed to bridge the gap between school and work that opened as unemployment rose. There were too many young people chasing too few jobs and, with the spread of adult unemployment, young people's lack of work experience prevented them acquiring this commodity that employers were able to demand. YOP was designed, and (when first introduced) appeared successful in creating sheltered occupations, thereby plugging the gap in the labour market that had opened as economic and technological trends plus adult competition closed school-leavers' opportunities (Ashton *et al.*, 1982). One economist, while querying the value of trainees' work to industry and the wider community, concluded that YOP was a highly effective scheme for alleviating youth unemployment quickly and cheaply (Metcalf, 1982). The programme was never intended to provide systematic vocational training. Those who hoped that YOP would become a permanent fixture envisaged the programme institutionalizing a period of vocational exploration with young people gaining experience of work tasks in work environments, while occupational identities and the status of employee were temporarily withheld until trainees had assessed their own abilities, acquired adequate knowledge of jobs and, therefore, were able to make rational choices (Watts, 1980). The MSC supported research and experiments to identify the most appropriate counselling arrangements for YOP trainees (Knasel, Watts and Kidd, 1982), including trainee-centred reviewing where young people themselves keep records of their experience and progress as an educational exercise, and as a basis for discussion with supervisors and careers officers (Pearce et al., 1981).

The programme appeared successful in enhancing its initial trainees' prospects of obtaining real jobs. Over 80 per cent gained employment within eight months of entering the programme. There were many instances of employers creating new jobs to retain trainees who had impressed supervisors while obtaining work experience. Other young people who were not retained in their work experience firms seemed to derive definite benefits. Many obtained jobs elsewhere during or soon after their six months training. They apppeared to have gained confidence and social skills in addition to work experience with which to impress prospective employers (Bayly, 1978; Bedeman and Harvey, 1981). All investigations among ex-trainees found that the majority evaluated YOP favourably (Smith and Lasko, 1978; Smith and Sugarman, 1981; Jones, Williamson, Payne and Smith, 1983). Even when young people failed to find employment immediately following their schemes, many were still grateful for the experience of life in industry, and off the dole.

It was observed, however, that the main determinant of success, obtaining a real job, was the level of unemployment prevailing in an area rather than any characteristics of the trainees or training themselves (O'Connor, 1981). As levels of adult and youth unemployment continued to rise, therefore, the proportion of trainees graduating to real jobs declined. In 1982 Sheffield Careers Service reported that only 20 per cent of YOP entrants could expect their schemes to lead to jobs. In Cleveland between October 1980 and January 1981 a mere 16 per cent of YOP trainees found proper employment. Researchers who explained how special measures preserved optimism in the search for work and cooled-out unrealistic aspirations, also noted that when training led straight back to the dole, cynicism spread rapidly and frustration increased (Driscoll, 1979; Jackson and Hanby, 1982).

Work experience on employers' premises was the most successful of YOP's components in leading to real jobs. This accords with experience in other countries. 'External' schemes are less successful than those which involve potential employers (Bresnick, 1982). However, when rising joblessness meant that even the schemes with the best prospects often led back to unemployment, employers' uses of work experience began attracting particularly vociferous criticism. These schemes were accused of exploiting young people as slave labour, filling shelves in supermarkets, serving in shops, and performing other jobs of value to the employers, for poverty 'wages'. Trade unions alleged substitution; that firms were using work experience instead of hiring wage earners. Young people complained that they were not offered genuine training.

Firms were able to retort that work experience was bound to involve a degree of substitution, that it was impossible to transform school-leavers into skilled workers within six months, and that they did not fix the allowances. Employers were not permitted to augment the basic allowance, though some failed to observe this regulation, with trainees' connivance. Firms saw no reason to conceal the value of work experience for screening potential recruits: one of the programme's aims was to give young people the opportunity to impress prospective employers. Whenever possible, individuals were offered work experience related to their eventual career intentions, which sometimes encouraged the young people to believe that they were being trained for employment as television engineers, motor mechanics or whatever, but YOP's aims were never so ambitious.

Community and project-based work experience rarely led directly to real jobs for the sponsors had none to offer, but these schemes possessed compensating features. The benefits of trainees' work were reaped by the wider community rather than private employers. Moreover, sponsors often insisted that 'trainees come first' (Brelsford *et al.*, 1981). Young people on community projects rarely complained of exploitation. Many appreciated their sympathetic and tolerant supervisors (Duffy, 1982).

There were suggestions that these schemes might be built into a national civil service to which all young people would be expected to commit a part of their lives but, as explained below, this was not the direction in which state measures eventually developed. There are powerful objections to a national civil service. Would the quality of the social services benefit from a massive influx of young, temporary and inexperienced workers, particularly if many felt conscripted? Should the wider society expect 'service' from young people? For most young people, community service would be a sidestep rather than a bridge. YOP was eventually replaced by a scheme that stressed 'training' rather than 'service', and aimed to distribute young people throughout the industries and firms in which they might spend their adult careers.

In general, work experience with a potential employer was more likely than any other youth opportunity to lead to permanent employment, but some external schemes built excellent track records, particularly the Information Technology Centres (ITECs). The Notting Hill Centre, the prototype, soon established a national reputation for turning unqualified school-leavers into sought-after recruits by firms seeking computer skills. By 1983, forty-one such centres were catering for approximately 1,000 trainees, mostly in deprived inner-urban areas, and some were generating income by marketing their services. Other external schemes which provided training in office skills, including the Sight and Sound courses, also established impressive placement records. But the very qualities that made these schemes successful in employers' eyes drew criticism from other quarters. The schemes were accused of training robot-like workers instead of a workforce versed in, and able to use, robotics.

The content of YOP remained basically unchanged, while the organizers' aims evolved during the programme's lifetime. It was not launched as a permanent fixture in the youth labour market. It was believed, in 1978, that the programme would need to expand until the early 1980s to accommodate growing numbers of school-leavers. Thereafter, as the numbers of school-leavers declined and the recession ended, it was envisaged that the programme would be phased down. Work experience was not meant to replace or compete with real jobs. In its early years, young people were only admitted to YOP once they had been registered as unemployed, seeking real jobs for at least six weeks:

> We must not lose sight of the fact that the ideal situation is one in which a young person gets a satisfactory job and does not enter the programme at all. If that aim is to be pursued, possible interference with the normal working of the labour market must be minimized. ... To make an opportunity available to every unemployed young person would be absurd and undesirable even if it were feasible, which, in our view, it is not.
> (Manpower Services Commission, 1977, p. 43)

Critics who have dismissed YOP as a palliative which merely papered over cracks in the economy instead of tackling a structural problem have enjoyed the benefit of hindsight. In 1978 no-one envisaged youth unemployment rising to the levels recorded in the early 1980s. By then the programme was being accused of trying to produce a de-politicized, compliant workforce by keeping young people in readiness for de-skilled jobs. Sceptics drew parallels with earlier (unsuccessful) attempts to provide compensatory education, and queried the implications in work experience and training in social and life skills that the young unemployed were at fault when, in reality, the failure leading to the spread of unemployment was on the jobs side of the labour market (Rees and Atkinson, 1982). Rather than being phased out, by the early 1980s the programme was being developed into a scheme offering initial vocational training for all 16-year-old school-leavers. In terms of these aspirations, YOP had many defects, despite the programme having exceeded the targets with which it was launched. When introduced in 1978 it was envisaged that, at a maximum, YOP would need to cater for 234,000 young people per year, the bottom third of school-leavers who neeeded a spell of work experience to strengthen their claims in competitive job markets. By 1982 the programme was handling over 550,000 trainees including the majority of 16-year-old school-leavers, not an uncompetitive minority, and most trainees were being returned to unemployment. The programme, like its predecessors, had been overwhelmed by the sheer scale of teenage joblessness.

The Young Workers Scheme

With YOP in crisis the government introduced new measures. In January 1982 the Young Workers Scheme (YWS) commenced. This offered employers a £15 weekly subsidy for 12 months per school-leaver hired at up to £40, and £7.50 if the wage was £40–£45. The aim was to encourage employers to hold down teenagers' wage rates, to make school-leavers cheaper and thereby encourage their recruitment. The scheme's advocates believed that one cause of youth unemployment was that, during the full-employment decades, beginning workers' wages had ceased to reflect their inexperience and that young people needed to price themselves back into the labour market. Subsidies were intended to reinforce market forces and speed the return of youth wages to 'realistic' levels. In the late 1960s and early 1970s, the gap between youth and adult wages narrowed whereas since 1976 it has widened, and since 1982 the YWS may have contributed to the depression of youth wage rates (Income Data Services, 1983).

When the YWS was introduced, the pay ceiling beneath which school-leavers attracted subsidies was above average earnings for beginning workers in most industries. As a result, many teenage jobs were subsidized; 101,500 during the scheme's first year. But it was estimated that only 11,500 of these jobs would not have been offered to young people if the subsidies were unavailable, and that 4,500 of the new youth jobs would otherwise have been taken by adults. In other words, only 7,000 additional jobs were created (*Guardian*, 1 June 1983). Deadweight is a problem with all general job subsidies. Much of the expenditure flows to jobs that would have been available irrespective of the schemes' existence. In the short-term, subsidies are far less effective in alleviating joblessness than schemes which create new opportunities outside conventional employment.

Job Splitting

In January 1983 a Job Splitting Scheme was introduced. This offered a financial inducement of £750 for every new post created as a result of former full-time jobs being split. During the recession, part-time employment had actually increased while full-time jobs were disappearing. The Job Splitting Scheme was an exercise in 'backing winners', investing in a growth area rather than attempting to preserve threatened full-time jobs. It was hoped that the total volume of employment would be enlarged, and that the trend towards part-time work would result in the number of individuals in jobs growing even more rapidly thereby achieving a significant fall in unemployment.

When the scheme was conceived it was envisaged that married women and workers approaching retirement might welcome the opportunity to become part-timers. It was also suggested that firms and trade unions might prefer job splitting to redundancies. A few firms had already split young people's jobs as a method of maintaining recruitment during the recession, but the scheme was not intended to set a trend towards part-time youth employment.

Young people would benefit indirectly if job splitting reduced general unemployment by redistributing work. The Job Release Scheme which allows older workers to retire before normal pensionable age, provided their jobs become available for young people, is another measure which aims to solve one group's unemployment by redistributing work from another. In 1983, 80,000 persons were benefiting from Job Release. However, these schemes have made little impression upon youth unemployment. By June 1983 the Job Splitting Scheme had supported the division of only 250 full-time posts. The next chapter explains why work sharing cannot be a satisfactory answer to unemployment. By 1983 the government had abandoned hope of restoring 16-year-olds' real jobs, and was planning to involve the entire age group in state-sponsored education or training.

The Youth Training Scheme

In 1981 the three-year-old YOP was already under attack for providing employers with slave labour, failing to offer genuine training and, therefore, often leading back to unemployment or, at best, unskilled jobs. Youthaid (1981) declared that unless its quality was improved the scheme would disintegrate as it lost credibility. The Manpower Services Commission's (1981a) response was to propose a New Training Initiative, the first stage being the replacement of YOP with a new Youth Training Scheme (YTS).

The 1979 Conservative government was described as 'ideological' and its Prime Minister as 'inflexible'. Yet they authorized the creation of a nationalized youth training industry without counterpart in any other non-communist country. The traditional view, endorsed by industry and successive British governments, was that training should be left to employers' discretion. Chapter 3 explained how this *laissez-faire* system survived the 1964 Industrial Training legislation and the 1973 Employment and Training Act which gave the MSC its statutory foundation. The Commission and government agreed that the former's Training Services Division should play a major role in adult retraining, but not in the initial training of beginning workers. The subsequent spread of youth unemployment swept traditions and ideological considerations aside. Through the YTS, which replaced YOP in 1983, the state is now committed to securing and monitoring initial vocational training for all 16-year-old school-leavers.

The YTS is an enlarged and enriched version of YOP. Youth training lasts a year compared with the normal six months on the earlier scheme, and sponsors are required to offer genuine training including at least 13 weeks off-the-job education rather than mere work experience. Another difference is that, rather than a solution to a temporary unemployment problem, the MSC regards the YTS as a permanent bridge from school to work.

In its first year the scheme endeavoured to cater for all otherwise unemployed 16-year-olds. In the longer term, the MSC intends the YTS to be the first instalment in a broader New Training Initiative (Manpower Services Commission, 1981a, 1981b, 1982). When proposing the scheme, the Commission recommended that the YWS, which subsidizes young people's jobs irrespective of their quality, should be phased out, so that all 16-year-old school-leavers could enter at least a year's planned training and part-time education. The government rejected this advice but accepted the aim of at least a year's training for all 16-year-old school-leavers by allowing young people to graduate from the YTS into

YWS-subsidized jobs. As a result, in most parts of Britain 16-year-olds now commence their working lives on allowances or wages around £25 per week, then compete for jobs where pay is held beneath the YWS ceiling. The affluent young worker has disappeared from most parts of Britain, but whether this extinction will lead to more jobs for teenagers remains uncertain. The failure of the YWS to revive youth employment during the scheme's first year, even if only by transferring jobs from other age-groups, reinforced doubts as to whether pay is a major determinant of demand for school-leavers, but the evidence remained inconclusive. Maybe the YWS will be more successful when it is not competing directly with a scheme that provides school-leavers free of charge to employers.

Since 1976, long before the YTS was envisaged, the Department of Education had been piloting Unified Vocational Preparation (UVP), with the intention of developing this scheme into a universal set of training and educational opportunities for young people (Department of Education and Science, 1979; Secretaries of State, 1979). School-leavers entering unskilled jobs, who formerly received neither further education nor training were the target group. UVP involved part-time college attendance integrated with on-the-job experience and lasted 6–12 months. Employers, trainees and tutors had all reacted favourably to the pilot schemes (Wray, Moor and Hill, 1980). If youth unemployment had never risen, it had been intended to expand UVP and realize the 1945 Ince Report's aspirations of offering basic vocational training and continuing education to all beginning workers. Mass youth unemployment changed the context but not the aim. The methods piloted on UVP have been available for absorption into the YTS. Once this scheme has been run in, all 16-year-olds who complete full-time education should proceed to at least a year's systematic training. In other words, the employment of 16-year-olds in ordinary jobs will be phased out.

As under YOP, youth training is offered in various modes. Many college, community, workshop and project-based schemes including the ITECs have been retained, sometimes enlarged and, where necessary, enriched to meet the higher standards of the YTS. However, like the older forms of work experience, youth training is normally on employers' premises. A difference is that under the YTS firms are allowed to give young people employee status and, if they wish, pay in excess of the basic allowance. It is expected that employment and extra pay will be negotiated by trade unions in some companies and/or offered by employers to attract 'better quality' school-leavers, particularly in areas where unemployment is relatively low or where there is a surplus of training places, and to secure the commitment of young people who are selected for retention following the initial year.

First-year apprentice training is eligible for inclusion in the YTS. Since 1983 this scheme has been the only source of public support for training young people, and as its training initiative develops the MSC intends to use financial support as a lever to persuade firms to improve the quality of apprentice training. Programmes will only qualify for support if they cover stipulated skills, and if entry is free from unnecessary age, gender and educational barriers:

> The provision of a broad-based initial year of training under the YTS should go a long way towards equipping young people to respond to change, and to retraining in their working lives.
> (Editorial, *Youth Training News*, April 1983, MSC).

No-one pretends that a year's basic training will meet all the economy's future skill requirements. As indicated above, if the MSC's full prospectus is adopted, the YTS will be just the initial stage in a longer-term New Training Initiative. Subsequent stages, if implemented, will expand and improve the quality of apprentice training, test trainees' competence, then develop training and retraining for adults. Following the initial year, the intention is that many young people will proceed to further 'accelerated' training, often as apprentices. Others, having been assisted by the scheme, are expected to win jobs in open competition, and to be capable of absorbing further training when opportunities arise and are sought at later stages in their careers. The training initiative could also be extended down the age-range with MSC sponsored technical education in schools as the foundation phase in integrated programmes for 14–18-year-olds.

The right approach?

At its birth, the YTS was guaranteed teething problems. The MSC needed 500,000 places. The co-operation of virtually all employers was sought through a publicity campaign and with an 'additionality rule', which made financial support conditional upon firms exceeding their normal recruitment. Five thousand places offered by the armed forces were gratefully accepted. Further education colleges had to gear themselves to an influx of youth trainees. Ensuring that all the latter received 'quality' training was bound to take time.

Simultaneously, the eventual success of the scheme, at least in gaining widespread acceptance, seemed assured. The YTS was approved by all

Britain's main political parties. By 1983 schemes were accepted by 16-year-olds in most areas as a necessary prelude to further training or real jobs. Schemes were also accepted by employers who had adjusted their recruitment strategies. Firms had seen the wisdom of meeting scheme requirements and having trainees' allowances plus overheads reimbursed by the MSC instead of hiring 16-year-olds at their own expense. When filling permanent jobs, industry had grasped the advantages of hiring 17- or 18-year-olds who had completed basic training successfully rather than raw school-leavers.

Needless to say, its likely survival does not necessarily mean that the YTS is the best of all possible initiatives. As explained below, the ways in which employers have learnt to use special measures are among contemporary school-leavers' problems. Having described how governments have responded to young people's employment difficulties, therefore, it may be useful to note what has not been done. Firstly, there has been no expansion of educational budgets. In the early 1980s recruitment into universities, colleges of higher education and polytechnics was actually curtailed. Sixteen-year-olds have not been tempted to remain in school with financial incentives, new courses or qualifications. Quite the reverse: they have been given financial incentives to terminate education despite the absence of jobs. If they become unemployed or enter special measures 16–18-year-olds receive state allowances, but not if they remain in education. The young unemployed lose entitlement to benefit if they register on full time further education courses, even if they are willing to accept jobs, should any become available. Unless 16-year-olds leave school at Easter and miss the summer examinations they cannot claim Supplementary Benefit until September. Since the mid-1970s the threat of unemployment has been persuading more girls to remain in education beyond the statutory leaving age. Among boys this trend only began after 1981 (Department of Education and Science, 1983). As a result, for the first time in British history the majority of young people are now staying on voluntarily. Unemployment has boosted enrolments in education, but this trend has occurred despite rather than in response to government policies. Catering for the 16-plus age group has been made a 'manpower' rather than an educational task. Policies to cope with youth unemployment have been hatched within the Department of Employment and the MSC rather than by the Department of Education and Science. In 1982 the task of sponsoring technical education for the 14–18-year-olds was entrusted to the MSC, not the teaching profession.

Secondly, between 1975 and 1983 there was no expansion of vocational training outside special measures. Financial support under the MSC Training for Skills Programme mitigated but did not reverse the loss of apprenticeships. There were no government initiatives to subsidize or otherwise expand apprentice training to cater for the increasing numbers of school-leavers, or to compensate for the loss of their ordinary jobs. Thirdly, attempts to generate ordinary employment for school-leavers including the YWS, have been unsuccessful, which is hardly surprising when, as explained below, it now appears that a side-effect of special programmes has been to squeeze real jobs from the market. Fourthly, local authorities and the Sports Council have targeted some projects at the young unemployed, but there has been no national programme to expand the youth, community and recreation services to provide jobless youth with some type of occupation.

Have government priorities been sound? Will the YTS provide school-leavers with new bridges, reshape the transition from school to work, and smooth the wider society's transition to advanced industrialism? Or would different initiatives prove more beneficial? It is not difficult to understand and defend the strategy that led to the YTS in 1983. Governments did not hand the unemployment problem to the leisure services because they intended to remove young people from, not reconcile them to joblessness. The employment side of school-leavers' bridges collapsed, so special measures were aimed at out-of-school youth, not those who remained in education. General subsidies for all youth jobs and/or apprenticeships would have involved considerable deadweight, especially when schemes were first introduced and youth unemployment was a minority problem. Pumping more money into existing training regimes would have perpetuated their defects. Subsidizing other youth jobs risked displacing unemployment to other age-groups. It seemed reasonable to introduce special measures which took school-leavers off the unemployment registers, off the streets and out of their homes where they might have succumbed to mischief or apathy, provided useful occupations, then left the young people better able to compete for real jobs.

The alarming growth of youth unemployment after the mid-1970s was unprecedented and unpredicted. There were no models to mimic. The initial special measures were inevitably experimental. Tactics were adjusted over time as programme organizers learnt from experience. Distributing young people throughout industry appeared preferable to congregating the young unemployed on separate projects. Successive measures emphasized training rather than the immediate value of the young people's work. If young people are still floundering, is this the fault of a fundamentally flawed strategy, or the result of recession deepening, demographic trends depositing increasing numbers of school-leavers onto the labour market, and unemployment mounting more rapidly than the strategy could be implemented? During the 1980s the demographic tide will turn. If and when general unemployment begins to fall, will the YTS accelerate the disappearance of youth unemployment? Will the scheme prove an effective bridge, allowing young people to make gradual transitions then embark upon adult careers capable of acquiring further skills?

Most research into special measures has been complimentary. Most of this research has been sponsored and published by the MSC. It has examined participants' views on the schemes, and measured their likelihood of leading to real jobs. On these criteria, all the schemes have appeared successful until overwhelmed by the scale of youth unemployment, whereupon the obvious solution has seemed to be to enlarge the measures. Will the YTS finally resolve their problems, or will it give a further twist to school-leavers' deteriorating prospects? By the time the YTS began operating in 1983 there were already suggestions, from the Labour Party and the EEC, that the training period would need extending from one to two years.

No-one has yet systematically examined the effects of state intervention not on participants' immediate prospects, but in the longer term on the structure of youth labour markets. When first introduced, the schemes were not intended to interfere with the normal operations of these markets, but they have now become a dominant feature. It is doubtful whether the recession coupled with longer-term changes in employers' recruitment strategies can account for the pace at which young people's jobs have disappeared since special measures were introduced. In 1982–3 the majority of 16-year-old school-leavers had to be accommodated on schemes. More resources have been devoted to tackling youth than adult unemployment, yet the former has continued to rise the more rapidly. Have policies for remedying youth unemployment supplied a classic case of an intended cure aggravating the problem under treatment? The successful marketing of YOP taught firms that there was no point in actually employing 16-year-olds when the latter's services could be obtained at no cost to the employer. An expectation was created that the state could and would cover initial training costs.

Early special measures helped to keep sub-employed youth afloat, but as schemes have been assimilated and helped to reshape youth labour markets they appear to have contributed to the destruction of school-leavers' real jobs while inflicting additional damage. They have transferred work from other age groups, thereby ensuring that youth trainees graduate from schemes into job-starved labour markets. Applying the Poor Law principle of 'less eligibility' to special measures, so that the terms and conditions are less attractive than the least-sought employment, has depressed the wages of young people who obtain real jobs. In 1982 16-year-old apprentices were paid around £39 per week and most school-leavers who obtained unskilled jobs received less (MSC, 1982). At the time, average pay for adult males was approximately £150. Young people's already modest starting rates have been undercut by state allowances. As explained earlier, since youth unemployment began rising the gap between teenage and adult earnings has widened, not narrowed. So much for the claim that young people, aided and abetted by trade unions, have been pricing themselves out of the labour market. Youth has ceased to be an affluent flowering period. Poverty standards are maintained in many households containing out-of-school children. Young parents, even if employed, are rearing young families on the minimum standards that the state deems tolerable.

A vicious 16-plus has been created, more divisive than the 11-plus ever was. Some young people are able to continue on the academic escalator. They are no longer required to defer gratifications. In absolute terms university graduates' qualifications have been devalued but, relatively speaking, higher education has become a more privileged route than ever. The academic elite has the immediate satisfaction of by-passing depressed youth labour markets. The prospects of the remainder often seem to depend on luck and employers' whims rather than objective attainments. Under the YTS as on YOP, schemes are being arranged in an informal hierarchy. Some are recognized as likely routes to real jobs. It is easy to understand the competition for places in firms that use the YTS as preliminary training and to select future technicians, office staffs and craft apprentices. Other young people find their 'training' excluding them from the pool that is allowed to compete for these 'good jobs'. This stratification of special measures has been observed in other countries. Australian programmes that earn good reputations are soon able to recruit the pick of local school-leavers, whereupon employers become keen that these schemes are not thrown open to all comers, including the long-term unemployed (Davis, 1982). The views of young people who experience the labour market as a lottery are easily understood. Life chances no longer hinge upon tests of ability at age 11, but they are often determined just as arbitrarily at age 16 or 17 in job and scheme interviews, and when supervisors judge whether individuals' performances during youth training have merited apprenticeships.

Vulnerable groups including the ethnic minorities and young people from unskilled working-class homes have received their fair share of places on government measures but, contrary to earlier hopes, the schemes have not reduced these school-leavers' disadvantages and thereby equalized opportunities, for the new routes usually act as warehouses and rarely lift young people up the labour market. Indeed, one study reports that ethnic minority youth who are disadvantaged in the search for real jobs have found their handicaps reinforced insofar as they tend to be placed on schemes with few prospects of leading to proper employment (Jones *et al.*, 1983). In time, Britain's new 16-plus will surely prove as controversial and unacceptable as the former segregation at 11 years of age.

7

Alternatives

The MSC's measures have many critics with no shortage of alternative policies which, for discussion and evaluation, can be divided into three groups.

Leisure solutions advise us to become reconciled to a long-term decline in employment and to solve our unemployment by operating on the 'supply side' of the labour market. Technology is displacing workers and, it is claimed, this trend will outlast the recession. Silicon chips and robots threaten jobs in most economic sectors. Some countries may develop new industries and actually expand employment by exploiting new technologies but, it is argued, only by exporting unemployment. According to this analysis, the only sure way of restoring full employment will be to reduce the supply of labour which will mean a growth of non-working time, or leisure.

Some advocate reduced hours and job splitting to provide work and leisure for everyone. Others envisage certain groups, probably the least qualified, least skilled and least productive never obtaining employment. An alternative would be to reduce pressure to seek employment among selected sections of the population thereby creating better job prospects for the remainder. Early retirement is currently encouraged by the Job Release Scheme. This encouragement could be extended by reducing the qualifying age for state pensions and increasing their value. Taxation and child benefit regulations could be manipulated to encourage more women with dependent children to become full-time housewives. Alternatively, young people could be withrawn from the labour market and offered a more leisurely adolescence. Is it perverse to respond to youth unemployment with education and training that reinforce work centrality in young people's expectations? Would it be more enlightened to nurture their leisure interests and offer access to recreation facilities?

Chapter 4 noted that Britain's unemployment rate in the 1980s has been well above average for western countries. There has been less discussion of the fact that Britain has more people actually in jobs per head of population than most other nations. Young people complete full-time education and seek jobs earlier, retirement ages are higher, and more married women hold employment in Britain than in many other countries. Does Britain really have a job-deficit problem, or is workaholism the real problem; are too many people trying to spend too much time in employment?

If persuaded to delay their entry into the workforce, young people could be offered a more varied menu than bread and circuses. Education could be prolonged and enriched with non-vocational objectives. Hargreaves (1982) proposes that comprehensive schools build a core curriculum around community studies and the expressive arts, teach pupils to work with and for groups, and how to reconcile their groups' interest with other's. Pressure to earn 'useful' qualifications could be eased by making job recruitment on the basis of educational credentials illegal, unless their relevance could be proved.

Maybe the wider society would be better advised to harness young people's energies to their unquestioned will to work. But if the quantum of employment destined to decline, thereby making a growth of leisure inevitable, the point holds that lasting solutions to unemployment must decide which sections of the public will be required and allowed to work, and for how many hours, then ensure that the remainder are offered sufficient income, alternative statuses and activities.

A second body of opinion advocates *vocational preparation*. It argues that future occupations will require more highly qualified and skilled workers than old-fashioned industrial jobs, that a smaller proportion of lifetime will be spent actually in employment, but that the time released will have to be devoted to education and training, maybe at repeated intervals, with working life divided into a series of consecutive careers. According to this analysis, the enlightened response to young people's current predicaments will be to develop the present youth unemployment industries into proper education and training provisions.

The withdrawal of children, then young people, from the workforce is not a recent development. The trend has been underway throughout industrial history. Two underlying processes have been responsible. First, changes in the economy and occupational structure have left firms unable to absorb huge armies of young, unskilled, inexperienced workers. Nineteenth-century employers protested that their enterprises would become unprofitable if denied child labour whereas modern industries cannot absorb hordes of young recruits. Secondly, young people have sought to delay their entry into the workforce while acquiring qualifications and skills to enable them, eventually, to enter the occupational structure at higher levels. It can be argued that youth unemployment has risen since the 1960s because these trends have become desynchronized and that turning back the clock, trying to arrest economic and occupational change, is not the best way of achieving re-alignment. Would it be more in keeping with historical trends to invest in education and training? Some commentators claim that an under-educated and under-trained workforce has been among Britain's persistent economic problems (Ginzberg, 1979). Maybe there was too much youth employment in the 1950s and 1960s and insufficient youth training and education. It can be argued that the spread of youth unemployment has underlined the need, and simultaneously created an opportunity to implement long-overdue reforms. Previous chapters explained that universal part-time education for the under-18s was envisaged in the 1918 Education Act, and that the 1945 Ince Report recommended training for all beginning workers.

Advocates of vocational preparation differ on the proper contributions of education and training. This debate is sometimes acrimonious because professionals' jobs and career prospects are at stake in addition to young people's welfare. 'Trainers' insist that the best vocational preparation occurs in work environments, sampling genuine jobs, learning by watching and talking to adult workers other than teachers. They argue that once in industry, young people can discover and impress employers with vocational talents unimpeded by artificial examination hurdles. 'Educators' reply that some vocational talents – general mechanical intelligence, understanding of principles, adaptability and, above all, the ability to learn—are more likely to be fostered in education than job-based training. In addition, they stress the desirability of making preparation for adulthood a basically educational task. Schools and colleges claim to cater for all young people's needs and interests—social, political and recreational as well as vocational. Courses in social and life skills, promoted by the MSC, are mistrusted insofar as the explicit intention is to fit young people into industry and society rather than to respond to young people's own needs, which could mean encouraging a critical, maybe politicized, view of existing institutions (Davies, 1979). In 1982 the MSC's prohibition of political education on YOP lent force to these criticisms.

However, educators are rarely anti-industry. Nor are most supporters of training opposed to education. The latter invariably propose day- or block-release. The arguments are about proportions and priorities. Should trainees be released for educational programmes selected by trainers? Or should students be despatched for work experience for educational as well as vocational purposes? Many educators favour vocational relevance and hope to promote economic growth, though not at the expense of individual development. Both trainers and educators support 'alternation,' with young people dividing their time between industry and colleges, making gradual transitions into employment and acquiring a first taste of 'continuing education' (Jeanperrin, 1979). Virtually all supporters of vocational preparation agree that the traditional end-on model of education, then training, followed by employment, is fast becoming obsolete, and that future skilled workers will need to withdraw repeatedly to refresh and update their skills and knowledge. However, they also agree that young people must be given a satisfactory foundation on which adult training and education can build.

A third solution to youth unemployment would return to full employment, revive the demand for rather than reduce the supply of labour, *restore young people's real jobs* and re-activate the right to work that politicians used to proclaim for all citizens, old and young. Rebuilding school leavers' opportunities to make traditional transitions at age 16 rarely finds favour among older commentators, but it would be many 16-year-olds' first choice. The route to instant popularity before audiences of unemployed youth is to demand that their jobs be returned. Most young people who leave school at the earliest opportunity regard all the alternatives—education, schemes and more generous social security payments, as consolation prizes.

My own view is that leisure solutions are unnecessary and unworkable, that economic, technological and occupational trends—reinforced by dissatisfaction with the 16-plus-will create pressure for more training and educational opportunities, but that a jobs initative will also be essential to prevent long-term youth unemployment becoming a permanent scar in disadvantaged areas. The following passages explain why, alone and unaided, neither education, job-based training nor employment are likely to prove universal panaceas. As in the past, solving school leavers' problems will involve blending the right mixtures and being prepared to alter the ingredients in response to further social and economic changes. One lesson we can learn from history is that in industrial societies there can be no final solution to young people's transition problems. The latter are endemic and solutions are always provisional.

Leisure

The idea that there is no other way of tackling youth unemployment than reconciling young people to joblessness or redistributing work from other age groups is based on one of two false assumptions. Firstly, leisure would be the only solution if there was but a finite amount of work to be undertaken which was nearing completion, meaning that the end of scarcity was imminent. This is manifestly ridiculous. Human wants appear capable of indefinite extension. If it is not being packaged into jobs, an absolute shortage of work is not the obstacle. Ecological limits to growth which we may now be pressing make no difference. Work will survive, conserving and recycling instead of destroying the earth's resources.

It is impossible to forecast exactly which skills, products and services will be in demand in ten or even five years time. Attempts to predict the future shape of the workforce always flounder on points of detail. No-one can anticipate future scientific discoveries and technological innovations. But workers in virtually all public services and voluntary organizations have little difficulty when asked to list work that is currently being left undone. Schools, careers offices and social work departments could use extra staff. Britain's highways, sewers and railroads need replacing or repairing. So do homes, hospitals and prisons.

A second mistaken assumption is to envisage machines performing a a growing proportion of jobs more efficiently than humans, then to imagine that this will sentence human workers to redundancy. This is demonstrably false. If a time ever arrived when machines performed all tasks more efficiently, which is an unlikely prospect, the optimum arrangement would not be to mechanize all jobs while humans stood idle, but to concentrate technology on those operations where its comparative advantage was greatest, and to employ humans elsewhere. The same principles explain why trade is advantageous to both countries even when one produces everything more efficiently and cheaply than the other.

In the past, as standards of living have risen, people have taken some of the benefits in additional free time—earlier retirement, longer vacations and shorter work weeks. It is likely that these trends will continue. But the processes responsible for this growth of leisure bear no resemblance to those creating involuntary unemployment where individuals seeking work cannot find jobs.

Leisure is not the only answer: it is not even a possible solution to unemployment. Redistributing the available work so that all job seekers obtain a fair share has a superficial appeal. Young people may be attracted by plans to abolish overtime, reduce normal hours, encourage earlier retirement and tempt married women to remain at home in order to leave more jobs for school leavers. But do ageing workers and women want to be eased from the workforce? Is joblessness tolerable when the victims are approaching retirement or female? Reducing hours spreads demand for labour only if real wages per hour are not raised in compensation. How many existing job holders wish to share their incomes? The existing Job Release and Job Splitting schemes have not restored school leavers' jobs.

It is possible, on paper, to argue youth out of economic existence. Present-day industry can survive without adolescent labour. It may no longer be technically necessary for youth to be spent in employment or even, in many cases, preparing for work in training or education. Youth could become literally spare time, relative to economic requirements, like old age. So why not offer adolescents a prolonged and leisurely education, or occupy them in recreation? Chapter 5 explained that leisure is only meaningful when part of a broader package. Education can prepare young people for work *and* leisure, but not the latter *instead* of the former. Offering the failures leisure education and services would reinforce their disadvantages. Moreover, it will be impossible to keep teenagers in a state of innocence, protected from the need, eventually, to compete for jobs.

Training

A real training initiative is a stronger candidate as a response to young people's immediate difficulties and longer-term occupational trends. Indeed, the MSC has argued the case for following the YTS with enlarged, enriched and properly monitored apprenticeships, plus better training for adults. If Britain is to attract and nurture growth industries based on new technologies, an appropriately trained workforce will be essential. If older industries are to survive they must re-equip with new machines and skills. None of this will be possible in Britain unless the collapse of training since the mid-1970s is reversed. The economic need will exist and young people are likely to seek further on-the-job training and sandwich schemes as alternatives to unskilled jobs or unemployment following their initial year.

The case for 'more training' encounters no principled opposition. This argument is one-sided. The matters under debate are who should provide, finance and receive training. Are the high apprenticeship countries—West Germany, Austria and Switzerland, suitable models for

Britain? In West Germany only 10 per cent of young people complete education at the earliest opportunity then receive no further training. The majority of school-leavers are apprenticed (Grimond, 1979). Industry offers near-universal opportunities: training is regarded as a right of young people and in firms' own interests. There are apprentice programmes combining on-the-job experience and education in over 400 occupations. Apprentices receive subsistence-plus-pocket-money allowances rather than adult wages. Government grants are available, but employers bear the greater share of training costs, which they partly or wholly recoup through their use of cheap apprentice labour. Many West German apprentices never practise the occupations in which they are trained, but it is argued that any training is better than none. Her apprentice system is credited with having given West Germany an adult workforce capable of rapid retraining in response to technological and occupational change, assisting the country to rise from military defeat to become the most powerful economy in Western Europe. Japan is another nation where firms systematically absorb and train virtually all beginning workers. These countries are frequently named as exemplars for others (Bresnick, 1982). Admirers hope that by sponsoring the YTS, then with more selective training grants, the MSC will spread a faith and willingness to invest in training that will lay similar foundations for economic growth and prosperity in Britain.

If training is a 'good thing', does it follow that 'the more the better' and that the best of all possible ways of re-organizing the transition into employment will be to train all young people? The 1945 Ince Report contained this recommendation. Britain's past industrial record might have been more successful had this proposal been implemented alongside other post-war reforms. Where they have existed, universal apprentice systems appear to have been recipes for success in the industrial past, but will the German model meet future needs? There are three objections.

First, training future skilled workers is likely to require higher educational levels than traditional craft apprenticeships. The key personnel in future growth industries and services will not offer craft-like skills. They will be designing and adapting new technologies for old and new products and markets. They will work in laboratories, drawing rooms, committees and task forces, with keyboards and print-outs rather than in traditional occupational communities. Training initiatives that endeavour to attract 16-year-olds from full-time education could prove self-defeating.

Secondly, the efficient use of resources surely requires selective rather than universal training. Will any worthwhile initiative involve the majority of employers? Can they all acquaint young people with technologies and techniques on which future economic success will depend? Instead of encouraging all firms to participate, it could be preferable to identify and use leading firms in different sectors as 'colleges'. The notions that all firms should undertake a fair share of training and that poaching is wicked were bred in an age of stable technology.

Should all beginning workers be trained? We are not all destined for occupations requiring expertise in the new information technologies. No-one envisages unskilled work disappearing. Indeed, the most advanced technologies create many routine operations demanding dexterity, attentiveness and experience, but not skill in the customary sense. Technological change is up grading some jobs while de-skilling and degrading others (Gorz, 1972; Braverman, 1974; Wood, 1982). Any training initiative, including Britain's YTS, is likely to lose credibility when it becomes apparent that many trainees face a choice between unemployment and unskilled jobs. Operatives can develop the qualities their jobs require by simply practising the occupations. Systematic training programmes that last years or even months are superfluous. Identifying generic manual skills like using scissors and screwdrivers, and social skills such as addressing questions to supervisors and colleagues, ensuring that they are included initial work experience, then checklisting trainees' performances as on the YTS, destroys the customary meanings of training and skill.

Another danger in training for employment that requires experience rather than genuine skill, particularly when employers recoup some costs through cheap apprentice labour, is displacing unemployment to other age groups. Special measures in Britain have grown alongside unemployment among the 18–25-year-olds. At the time of writing, in 1983, West Germany has rising unemployment among former apprentices in their early twenties. Universal training may offer only a temporary refuge from unemployment.

Third, transplanting institutions is never straight forward. West German employers and trade unions believe that training is a 'good thing'. Grimond (1979) has argued that if apprentice wages are low enough and if trade unions will co-operate, British industry's self-interest will generate near-universal training opportunities. He is wrong. British employers do not share West Germans' customary faith that training will pay for itself and serve everyone's interests. Despite beginning workers' wages having fallen to subsistence levels it is the MSC, not private enterprise, that has supplied the cash and organizational drive to launch the New Training Initiative. In its early proposals the Manpower Services Commission (1981a) stressed the benefits of training to employers and young people who, it was argued, should bear most of the costs. Later 'realistic' recommendations stressed the public benefits and made the case for public funding Manpower Services Commission (1981b, 1982). Developing training in Britain will probably require higher levels of public spending and stronger public administration than in existing high apprenticeship countries.

Education

It is impossible to say exactly when, but at some point educational growth must resume unless economic growth is to become just a historical phenomenon. Any expansion of employment in high technology industries and services will boost demand for educated manpower. In any event, young people and parents will demand opportunities to acquire qualifications that lead to good jobs.

Everyone realizes that expansion will require structural change, but there are different views on how education should be reformed. A currently influential body of opinion insists that a major problem with British education is its lack of relevance, especially vocational relevance. Curiously, those who voice this criticism often propose to leave the least relevant courses, the academic roads through 'A'-levels towards higher education, intact and create new vocational tracks for non-academic youth. The aims are laudable: to replace the frustrating experience of struggling for, then failing, CSEs and to enhance young people's employability (Grimond, 1979), but the strategy will fail. The idea is not new. Britain tested it in secondary modern schools. France and the USSR give young people the option of completing their schooling on vocational courses. We know how these schemes work in practice.

British advocates of a vocational track envisage parity of esteem with academic programmes, which is as likely as equal status between secondary moderns and grammar schools. In 1982 the Labour Party's education spokesman warned that the technical courses for 14–18-year-olds, to be supported by the MSC, would roll back the comprehensive principle and exhume the secondary moderns. The courses will fail for identical reasons. Their supporters envisage vocational tracks recruiting bright and eager young people who are keen to acquire technical skills, the bait that employers will snatch. Where they exist, vocational courses tend to be unpopular and under-subscribed. They recruit students with no choice, who lack ambition or ability. These young people are avoided by employers, except for jobs no-one else wants, if there are any. Like other special measures, vocational courses are obviously intended for other people's children. Independent schools are well-exposed by market pressures. How many are developing vocational tracks? Bipartite secondary education, and the intention that CSEs should be taken only by the remainder of the top 50 per cent who found 'O'-levels too demanding were undermined by the unwillingness of parents and pupils to settle for second best. In the 11-plus era, primary schools were judged by their passes. If separate academic and technical streams are established within comprehensives, these schools will be judged by the proportions enrolled on academic courses. Parents who believe their children stand any chance will insist on them competing for first prizes, and schools will feel unable to withhold the opportunity.

Vocational tracks are a response to the long-rehearsed but ill-founded criticism of education for failing to offer vocational preparation that is only possible once individuals have entered employment. Whatever they say when interviewed, employers do not act on the expectation that school-leavers should possess vocational skills. They use credentials as proof of general ability, industriousness and, above all, a capacity to learn. In the future as in the past, students will seek qualifications that employers reward, and providing these opportunities will mean widening the mainstream, thereby allowing a higher proportion of young people to qualify and undertake training in the skills that future growth industries and services will demand.

The main structural reform required to unblock British education's mainstream is in the public examinations at 16-plus. These exams were designed to weed out all but a talented few. It is inevitable that the majority fail and are left with nowhere to travel up the educational ladder. As Wilby (1979) argues, the main problem with Britain's comprehensives is that their standards are artificially high rather than too low. The most radical proposals for opening opportunities at 16-plus would abolish public examination at this age and design curricula on the assumption that young people will remain in education until age 17 or 18. Other proposals would merge 'O'-levels and CSEs, then replace 'A'-levels with an examination within the majority's capacities. Sweden and the USA have broad-based mainstreams that encourage all young people to remain in full-time education at least until age 18.

Having opened the mainstream it will be possible to inject some of the relevance that the vocational track's supporters seek by revising traditional notions of ability, rewriting curricula, and ceasing to treat the abstract as more worthy than the applicable. Husen (1978) argues that instead of catering for different levels of ability, contemporary schools need to educate different *kinds* of talent and recognize society's need for multiple skills. After such a genuinely comprehensive secondary educa-

tion, young people could move into comprehensive university or polytechnic *systems* offering full- and part-time courses for students with
many kinds of interests and abilities (Burgess, 1977; Pedley, 1977).

There would be no need to confine these wider opportunities within
conventional schools. Education could be invigorated with additional
students, curricula and methods, including some alternatives urged by
deschoolers (Illich, 1971; Reimer, 1971). New information technologies
create a need for a more highly educated workforce, and simultaneously
threaten the schools' educational monopoly (Froyland, 1980). Community education outside schools, incidental education, a by-product of
participating in work, recreational and community organizations, and
free schools where attendance is voluntary and students can opt in at
any time to proceed at their own pace, could prove more attractive to
many young adults than conventional lecture halls and classrooms.
These alternatives are unlikely to be universally welcomed. We have
been warned that young people whose backgrounds supply relevant
skills and motivations will derive the greatest benefits, and that the deschoolers' reforms would deepen social divisions (Barrow, 1978). However, these dangers could be lessened by offering alternative programmes
alongside, as options, rather than replacing familiar forms of education.
Wider educational opportunities at 16-plus may not break the link
between social origins and eventual attainments, but they would make
it impossible for young people to fail irrevocably or earn lifetimes of
privilege before even completing compulsory schooling.

Opportunities to continue in education need not be restricted to 16-
year-olds. As previously explained, the idea that education and training
are splendid for the young but unnecessary for adults is obsolete. Educational vouchers have been debated as a means of giving parents greater
choice, and exposing primary and secondary schools to market pressures. There is a stronger case for issuing vouchers to everyone completing compulsory schooling, which would cover maintenance and course
costs for a given number of years in education or training at any point in
the life cycle. Would it be in their own or the wider society's interest if
everyone cashed these vouchers before age 21? Secondary school pupils
and teachers find work experience a valuable stimulus. A taste of real
work prior to continuing education or professional training can make
educational and economic sense, in addition to matching many young
people's preferences. All researchers who have studied unemployed
youth report that the young people's first request is for jobs. However,
by their early twenties many of these same individuals have reconsidered.
They would grasp educational and training opportunities if any were
available and within their means.

A danger when listing all the possible innovations is of portraying education as a solve-all, capable of absorbing everyone whose labour power is temporarily dispensable, offering meaningful experiences and, eventually, opening attractive careers. These rewards will remain elusive, and if such careers are the prize education will remain competitive. Non-vocational objectives including the cultivation of leisure interests and skills will be admissible alongside, but will not replace the pursuit of credentials. Indeed, post-compulsory education will become more, not less competitive if selection is transferred from earlier stages.

Education has not been responsible for the destruction of young people's former routes into working life, and educational reform alone will not rebuild their bridges. It is unrealistic to anticipate all young people seeking more education. Experience in other countries suggests that it will be impossible to retain all 16-year-olds. Some would drop out for practical purposes even if the statutory leaving age was raised however relevant, varied and attractive the courses. Moreover, we know that the young people who are least likely to take advantage of wider educational opportunities are the same individuals who are currently at greatest risk of unemployment—unqualified early school-leavers. In other words, those in the greatest need are the least likely to assisted by educational reform and growth. It may be argued that if the majority of young people are retained in education there will be sufficient jobs for the remainder. In practice this situation could create new dangers. When the drop-outs are a tail-end of failures, as in the USA, employers avoid them when recruiting to 'good jobs'.

Over-enthusiastic educational expansion, running ahead of economic growth and occupational trends, can swell unemployment among highly educated young adults. Many Third World and some European countries including Spain, Italy and Greece already face mass graduate unemployment. It is possible to educate young people to levels that make them unattractive to employers who do not expect well-qualified recruits to settle and work co-operatively in the available jobs, while the young people are equally reluctant to compromise their aspirations (Roberts, 1981b).

Jobs

There are three reasons for believing that, in addition to wider educational and training opportunities, a jobs initiative will eventually prove essential. Firstly, the credibility of any educational and training programmes, whatever their quality, will be undermined if substantial numbers graduate to unemployment. Secondly, as argued earlier, un-skilled and de-skilled jobs will not disappear. Young people who realize they are not to become highly qualified and skilled technocrats will dismiss education and training as pointless. Recruiting these young people will create control problems for teachers and trainers without upgrading the workforce. Generations of school-leavers have proved that the generic abilities required in unskilled employment can be ac-quired perfectly adequately in real jobs without simulated scheme ex-perience. Thirdly, even if deferred gratifications are visible, there will always be some 16-year-olds who prefer immediate independence, adult status and real wages, however low, to education or formal training. Unless youth employment is made illegal, and maybe even then, there will always be employers willing to hire cheap school-leavers, and many 16-year-olds who have spent years longing for their release from class-rooms are sufficiently mature to cope with unemployment, if necessary, while seeking these jobs. Young people in Britain are neither so uni-formly apathetic nor demoralized as to gratefully accept whatever alter-natives their elders recommend.

In many countries, the spread of youth unemployment has been accompanied by concern at special programmes failing to reach—or merely scratching—the surface of the 'real problem group', the young people at greatest risk of joblessness. Some disappear on terminating full-time education when they lose contact with statuory agencies with-out any known occupational destinies. Sometimes the young people are unaware of the opportunities they are missing (Davis, 1982). Others are only too aware that, given the chance, the statutory agencies will pressure them into schemes (Roberts *et al.* 1981). Long-term youth unemployment will become a long-term problem unless sufficient jobs are generated to absorb young people who will reject any alternatives. If society fails to supply these jobs, it will find itself bearing the costs of managing instead of curing persistent long-term unemployment in disadvantaged, often multi-racial areas. Must law enforcement and welfare be these districts' only growth industries?

Supporters of young people's right to work encounter two objections. First, it is argued that conceding this right will be contrary to young people's own long-term interests because if unskilled employment con-tinues to contract, as forecasters predict, school-leavers who receive no training or further education could be trapped in secondary labour markets, to spend their entire lives chasing a diminishing number of jobs without the means to climb into more secure and better-paid employ-ment. The second objection is that while, in theory, there may be plenty of work to be done, we lack mechanisms to transform this work into jobs quickly enough to assist even the 1990s' school-leavers. Plans for economic recovery that include job subsidies of up to £70 a week per additional worker hired do not envisage unemployment falling beneath 1,000,000 within the foreseeable future (Layard, 1981). Employers' preferences station young people towards the end of the queue. If young people's jobs were heavily subsidized, or their wages even more severely depressed than currently, employers' preferences might change, but if this created jobs for young people it could be at the expense of higher unemployment in other age groups. In Denmark employees over age 18 are covered by minimum wage legislation. The under-18s are relatively cheap and fully employed, whereas unemployment has risen steeply in the 18-plus age group. Do we want to create more blind alleys in Britain?

The paternal case for withholding young people's right to work in their own long-term interests is easily rebutted. The shape of the occupational structure means that some individuals will have to perform unskilled jobs whatever opportunities school-leavers are offered or denied. It has been commonplace in Britain to deplore the large numbers of young people who—in the past—drifted into, then between, unskilled jobs. Were all the young people damaged? With time and experience the majority gravitated into better-paid, more secure occupations. Drifting between jobs is a proven means of acquiring generic work skills and habits, experience, flexibility and adaptability. Many initially unskilled workers acquire skills informally, by dilution. Improved access to adult training and education could widen opportunities for career mobility. It is not their own interests but their powerlessness that has driven teenagers from their former jobs. They are vocationally inexperienced and therefore lack economic power. They are political lightweights. The under-18s have no votes. Young people have never been mobilized on youth issues. Governments have been able to stand by, maybe connive, in the destruction of young people's jobs without suffering electorally.

If orthodox reflation will not deliver sufficient jobs, must we learn to live with the shortfall or set about supplementing orthodox reflation? There are plenty of public work programmes as candidates for expansion. Community organizations that have co-operated on existing special measures have demonstrated how needs can be met by transforming voluntary work into paid employment. Job generation in high unemployment areas might accelerate if more schools, colleges and training schemes nurtured entrepreneurial skills and equipped young people to become employers as well as employees. Companies employing less than 200 account for 28 per cent of manufacturing jobs, and these small businesses are not declining. In Britain and America large firms have been cutting their workforces while employment in small businesses has actually increased.

Risks and opportunities

School- and scheme-leavers are still floundering not because we lack ideas or even the resources to act decisively provided new educational, training and job opportunities are built gradually, step by step. The impediments are political: summoning the will and, in particular, securing agreement on how resources should be marshalled.

How and why school-leavers' former bridges have collapsed is not mysterious. Once the evidence is assembled the explanations are clear. No serious students of the topic are perplexed. Nor is it difficult or even controversial to identify the measures that reconstruction will require. There are arguments over whether leisure solutions have any merit, exactly how many young people should be absorbed in different types of education and training, and how many will be best served by real jobs, but I have yet to encounter any body of informed opinion which disputes that repairing the transition into employment will require a mixture of educational, training and jobs initiatives built around, or eventually replacing the YTS. Deciding what opportunities to offer to young people is the current problem, if the latter term fits, for facing this dilemma must be considered an advance on the situation where the majority of 16-, 15- and, before then, 14-year-olds could be given no alternative but to begin lifetimes in unrewarding jobs from which, in most cases, there could be no escape, except for women into unpaid domestic labour.

Everyone claims to deplore youth unemployment and the aimlessness of marking time in schemes and courses leading nowhere in particular. The transition into employment has been a problem requiring special measures since 1975. Everyone agrees that the problem is structural, that economic recovery alone will not resolve school-leavers' difficulties and that, in the long term, failure to provide better opportunities for beginning workers will jeopardize economic development. So why has there been no comprehensive attempt to re-shape education, training and youth employment to restore smooth transitions?

Consensus collapses when the debate considers how to marshall the resources to develop education and training, and to generate new jobs. All proposals have implications for the type of society future generations will inhabit, they all arouse fears that outweigh enthusiasm, and the net result is political paralysis.

On the right, a massive expansion of state education and training is judged an unacceptable threat to freedom and enterprise. So how are the opportunities that young people will seek and that the economy needs to be created? Some families will ensure that their young people receive whatever training and education are necessary to enter progressive careers. Free marketeers argue that these families must be allowed to remain on their own feet without the tax burden that rising public spending implies. They argue that, provided profits are allowed to stay in entrepreneurs' hands, the rewards of commercial success will persuade firms to support relevant education and training. Simultaneously, it is argued, the incentive of career rewards will persuade growing numbers of young people and parents to invest in, develop and profit from their talents. Eventually it is envisaged that the urge to 'get on' will draw the majority into prolonged education and/or training, then into the well-paid jobs that a dynamic economy will generate. State support for education and training would be used to reinforce the market, supplementing and encouraging but not replacing the investments of firms and individuals.

This is one way whereby, given time, school leavers' bridges could be rebuilt, but no-one can be certain that the strategy will succeed. There are formidable risks. The end-product could be a deeply divided society with a highly qualified minority drawing internationally competitive salaries, while a large working class held onto its traditional jobs and wage-levels above a growing underclass, relegated to the margins of the workforce or careers as claimants. Some would welcome and benefit from these divisions. Others reject even the risk.

An alternative strategy would enlarge education, training and, if necessary, subsidized employment. Ensuring that all young people found jobs, education or training opportunities would become public responsibilities. The most generous prospectuses would guarantee all 16-year-olds an income, recreation and even independent accommodation as well as education, training or employment. Standard grants or allowances— maybe graduated by age, and certainly supplemented according to need to prevent young families and children struggling in poverty—would be available for all, whatever types of education or training they entered.

Would this mean socialism by stealth? Many advocates of greater public support for education and training at 16-plus deny revolutionary intentions. They insist that they are not seeking to replace the market, abolish private property or restrict free enterprise. Indeed, they can claim that their intentions are thoroughly conservative. The state has become a provider of universal elementary, then secondary, education. Why should there be principled objections to universal provision at the tertiary level? The problems of school-leavers in the 1980s are particularly acute but, it can be argued, they are not fundamentally different from previous generations'. Young people have always been peripheral to the work-force, buffeted by successive changes. In the past, transitional arrange-ments have been changed repeatedly, usually by providing better jobs, more education or training. The reforms required in the 1980s may prolong adolescence but his life phase between childhood and adulthood is not novel, and likewise enlarging public education and training will extend rather than depart from existing practices. If investment in youth education and training paid for itself in the long term, state spending could increase without consuming a growing share of the gross national product. If the public share did increase marginally, would this involve any radical change in an already mixed economy? It can be argued that extending public support to the 16-plus age group will consolidate a healthy long-term trend towards greater social equality and democracy without threatening political liberties or economic freedom.

If prolonged education and training cease to involve financial sacrifice, it will become difficult to justify the pay differentials that qualifications have earned in the past. In any case, changes in the shape of the occupa-tional structure seem certain to erode these differentials. When the majority of workers are in white-collar service occupations they cannot all be paid above-average salaries. It is not blue-collar trade unionists' wage expectations that have burdened the economy with inflationary pressures. Their take-home pay has been held down as more-and-more have become income tax payers as a result of governments' failure, over the last 30 years, to index tax allowances. It is managements and profes-sions seeking to maintain historical differentials who are refusing to live in a changing real world.

Some would applaud, not grieve, if state intervention to rebuild young people's bridges meant the downfall of capitalism. They argue that the spread of youth unemployment is a symptom of capitalism's latest, may-be final, crisis. Might this latest contradiction between the measures required to reproduce the workforce and the profits necessary to sustain the system, prove fatal? At some point, rising social consumption in education, training and other spheres must squeeze profits and income differentials, and stifle their pursuit. If the only answer is for state to direct investment, prohibit the export of capital, and socialize production alongside consumption, some will welcome the prospect. Others, how-ever, seek to avoid this future at all costs, even the persistence of youth and adult unemployment. Meanwhile even capitalism's critics must admit lacking any guarantee that socialist planners will prove more competent than market forces in generating economic growth, predicting skill requirements and meeting young people's aspirations.

All possible methods of harnessing resources to rebuild school-leavers' bridges involve risks. Neither the free marketeers nor state intervention-ists can be confident that their visions will become realities. Nor can they be certain of the fearful consequences they associate with opponents' strategies. Hence the political attractions of muddling through. This may distil the best, but it could leave Britain with the worst of all possible outcomes. In a competitive world some countries or trading blocks must win. Their human resource policies will assist some countries in develop-ing new industries and services that enable them to become leading post-industrial economies. Others are likely to enter the twenty-first century struggling to maintain their traditional industries, jobs and standards of living. Is the YTS preparing school-leavers for this type of future? Periods in waiting rooms, temporary jobs and unemployment could prove an admirable preparation for adult careers as claimants, or on the margins of a declining economy's workforce.

Bibliography

Abrams, M. (1961) *The Teenage Consumer,* London Press Exchange, London.

Adams, D. and Sawdon, D. (1978) 'In and out of work', *Actions,* January 1978.

Albermarle Report (1960) *The Youth Service in England and Wales,* HMSO, London.

Allen, S. and Smith, C.R. (1975) 'Minority group experience and the transition from school to work', in Brannen, P. (ed.) *Entering the World of Work,* HMSO, London.

Anderson, N. (1967) *Work and leisure,* Routledge and Kegan Paul, London.

Ashton, D.N. and Field, D. (1976) *Young Workers,* Hutchinson, London.

Ashton, D.N. and Maguire, M.J. (1980a) 'Young women in the labour market: stability and change', in Deem, R. (ed.) *Schooling for Women's Work,* Routledge and Kegan Paul, London.

Ashton, D.N. and Maguire, M.J. (1980b) 'The functions of academic and non-academic criteria in employers' recruitment strategies', *British Journal of Guidance and Counselling,* 8, 146–157.

Ashton, D.N., and Maguire, M.J. (1982) 'The organisation of local labour markets: Dual markets or market segments'; Paper presented to workshop on The Manangement and Mismanagement of Labour, Loughborough University.

Ashton, D.N., Maguire, M.J. and Garland, V. (1982) *Youth in the Labour Market,* Research Paper 34, Department of Employment, London.

Association of Recreation Managers (1981) 'Recreation programmes for the unemployed—do they work?', in *The Changing Scene: Seminar Report,* ARM, St Annes-on-Sea.

Ball, C. and Ball, M. (1979) *Fit For Work?* Writers and Researchers Publishing Co-operative, London.

Barrow, R. (1978) *Radical Education,* Martin Robertson, London.

Baxter, J.L. (1975) 'The chronic job-changer: a study of youth unemployment', *Social and Economic Administration,* 9, 184–206.

Bayly, L.P. (1978) *The Work Experience Programme,* Manpower Services Commission, London.

Bazalgette, J. (1978) *School Life and Work Life,* Hutchinson, London.

Becker, H.S. and Carper, J.W. (1956a) 'The development of identification with an occupation', *American Journal of Sociology*, 61, 289-298.

Becker, H.S. and Carper, J.W. (1956b) 'The elements of identification with an occupation', *American Sociological Review*, 21, 341-348.

Becker, H.S. and Carper, J.W. (1957) 'Adjustments to conflicting expectations in the development of identification with an occupation', *Social Forces*, 36, 51-56.

Becker, H.S. *et al.* (1963) *Boys in White*, University of Chicago Press.

Bedeman, T. and Harvey, J. (1981) *Young People on YOP*, Manpower Services Commission Research and Development Series, 3, London.

Beetham, D. (1967) *Immigrant School-leavers and the Youth Employment Service in Birmingham*, Institute of Race Relations, London.

Bellaby, P. (1977) *The Sociology of Comprehensive Schooling*, Methuen, London.

Beloe Report (1960) *Secondary Examinations other than GCE*, Ministry of Education, HMSO, London.

Benn, C. and Simon, B. (1970) *Half-Way There*, McGraw-Hill, London.

Berg, I. (1973) *Education and Jobs*, Penguin, Harmondsworth.

Bevington, S. (1933) *Occupational Misfits*, Allen and Unwin, London.

Bhroin, N.B. (1970) *The Motivation and Productivity of Young Women Workers*, Irish National Productivity Committee, Eire.

Birksted, I.K. (1976) 'School performance viewed from the boys', *Sociological Review*, 24, 63-77.

Boles, J.M. and Garbin, A.P. (1974) 'The choice of stripping for a living', *Sociology of Work and Occupations*, 1, 110-123.

Bowles, S. and Gintis, H. (1976) *Schooling in Capitalist America*, Routledge and Kegan Paul, London.

Braverman, H. (1974) *Labour and Monopoly Capital*, Monthly Review Press, New York.

Brelsford, P., Rix, A. and Smith, G. (1981) *Trainees Come First*, Manpower Services Commission Research and Development Series, 4, London.

Bresnick, D. (1982) 'The youth unemployment policy dance', paper presented to the American Political Science Association, Denver.

Brooks, D. and Singh, K. (1978) *Aspirations Versus Opportunities*, Commission for Racial Equality, London.

Bunker, N., Dewberry, C. and Kelvin, P. (1983) 'Unemployment and the use of time', *Leisure Studies Association Newsletter Supplement*, 1, 6-7.

Burgess, T. (1977) *Education After School*, Gollancz, London.

Burgess, T. and Pratt, J. (1974) *Polytechnics: A Report*, Pitman, London.

Cameron, C., Lush, A. and Meara, G. (1943) *Disinherited Youth*, Carnegie Trust, Edinburgh.

Careers Bulletin (1978) 'Employment problems of young people from ethnic minority backgrounds', *Careers Bulletin*, Autumn, 23-28.

Careers Bulletin (1982) 'First employment of young people', *Careers Bulletin*, Spring, 14-17.

Carmichael, D.M. (1976) 'Work experience', *Careers Quarterly*, 28, 26-34.

Carr Report (1958) *Training for Skill*, Ministry of Labour, HMSO, London.
Carter, M.P. (1962) *Home, School and Work*, Pergamon Press, Oxford.
Carter, M.P. (1966) *Into Work*, Penguin, Harmondsworth.
Cashmore, E. (1979) *Rastaman*, Allen and Unwin, London.
Casson, M. (1979) *Youth Unemployment*, Macmillan, Basingstoke.
Central Advisory Council for Education (1954) *Early Leaving*, HMSO, London.
Central Policy Review Staff (1978) *Social and Employment Implications of Microelectronics*, HMSO, London.
Central Policy Review Staff (1980) *Education, Training and Industrial Performance*, HMSO, London.
Centre for Contemporary Cultural Studies (1981) *Unpopular Education*, Hutchinson, London.
Chamberlain, J. (1983) 'Adolescent perceptions of work and leisure', *Leisure Studies*, 2, 127–138.
Cherry, N. (1976), 'Persistent job-changing—is it a problem?' *Journal of Occupational Psychology*, 49, 203–221.
Ching, J.E. (1970) 'Educational and vocational guidance for the able pupil *Careers Quarterly*, 22, 18–24.
Chown, S.M. (1958) 'The formation of occupational choice among grammar school pupils', *Occupational Psychology*, 32, 171–182.
Clark, B.R. (1960) 'The cooling-out function in higher education', *American Journal of Sociology*, 65, 569–576.
Clarke, L. (1977) *The Practice of Vocational Guidance: A Review of the UK Research Literature*, Report 35, Employment Services Agency, London.
Clarke, L. (1980a) *Occupational Choice: A Critical Review of Research in the United Kingdom*, HMSO, London.
Clarke, L. (1980b) *The Transition for School to Work: A Critical Review of Research in the United Kingdom*, HMSO, London.
Clements, R.V. (1958) *The Choice of Careers by School-children*, Manchester University Press.
Closs, J., Downs, S. and Willoughby, J. (1977) 'Me Tarzan, you Jane', *Careers Quarterly*, 28, 4, 24–31.
Colledge, M., Llewellyn, G. and Ward, V. (1977) *Young People at Work*, Manpower Services Commission, London.
Collins, R. (1979) *The Credential Society*, Academic Press, New York.
Commission for Racial Equality (1978) *Looking for Work*, London.
Community Relations Commission (1974) *Unemployment and Homelessness: A Report*, HMSO, London.
Conant, J.B. (1965) 'Social dynamite in our large cities: Unemployed out-of-school youth', in Kerber, A. and Bommarito, B. (eds.) *Schools and the Urban Crisis*, Holt, Rinehart and Winston, New York.
Cox, C.B. and Dyson, A.E. (eds.) (1969) *Fight for Education: a Black Paper*, Critical Quarterly Society, London.
Crowther Report (1959) *15–18*, Central Advisory Council for Education, HMSO, London.

Daniel, W.W. and Stilgoe, E. (1976) 'Towards an American way of unemployment', *New Society*, 12 February 1976.
Daniel, W.W. and Stilgoe, E. (1977) *Where are They Now?* Political and Economic Planning, London.
Davies, B. (1979) *In Whose Interests?* National Youth Bureau, Occasional Paper 19.
Davis, D.J. (1982) *Youth, Jobs and Education Programmes in Western Sydney*, New South Wales Department of Environment and Planning.
Department of Education and Science (1977) *Education in Schools: a Consultative Document*, HMSO, London.
Department of Education and Science (1979) *A Better Start in Life*, HMSO, London.
Department of Education and Science (1983) 'Educational and economic activity of young people age 16 to 19 years in England and Wales from 1973-4 to 1981-2', *Statistical Bulletin*, February 1983.
Department of Employment (1970) *At Odds*, HMSO, London.
Department of Employment (1981) *A New Training Initiative: a Programme for Action*, HMSO, London.
Dex, S. (1982) *Black and White School-leavers*, Department of Employment Research Paper 33, London.
Donovan, A. and Oddy, M. (1982) 'Psychological aspects of unemployment: an investigation into the emotional and social adjustment of school-leavers', *Journal of Adolescence*, 5, 15-30.
Dore, R. (1976) *The Diploma Disease*, Allen and Unwin, London.
Douglas, J.W.B. (1964) *The Home and the School*, McGibbon and Kee, London.
Douvan, E.A. and Adelson, J. (1966) *The Adolescent Experience*, John Wiley, New York.
Driscoll, J. (1979) 'Training to be on the dole again?' *Youth in Society*, 33, 9-10.
Driver, G. (1980), 'How West Indians do better at school (especially the girls)', *New Society*, 17 January 1980.
Duffy, J.A. (1982) *A Community and Business Approach to Youth Unemployment*, Action Resource Centre, London.
Dungate, M. (1982) *Training Workshops*, Manpower Services Commission, Research and Development Series 8, London.
Eagar, W.M. and Secretan, H.A. (1925) *Unemployment Amongst Boys*, Dent. London.
Edwards, K.H.R. (1960) *The Secondary Technical School*, University of London Press.
Eggleston, J (1979) *The implications of school-to-work programmes for the development of vocational identities* (mimeo), OECD, Paris.
Elder, G.H. (1974) *Children of the Great Depression*, University of Chicago Press.
Employment Gazette (1978) 'The young and out of work', *Employment Gazette* August, 908-916.

European Economic Commission (1979) *Chomage et recherche d'un emploi; attitudes et opinions des publics Europeens*, EEC, Brussels.

Ferguson, T. and Cunnison, J. (1951) *The Young Wage Earner*, Oxford University Press.

Ferguson, T. and Cunnison, J. (1956) *In Their Early Twenties*, Oxford University Press.

Figueora, P. (1970) 'School-leavers and the colour barrier', *Race*, 506–507.

Fleming Report (1944) *Report of the Committee on Public Schools*, HMSO, London.

Flude, R.A. (1977) 'The development of an occupational self-concept and commitment to an occupation in a group of skilled manual workers', *Sociological Review*, 25, 41–49.

Flude, R.A. and Whiteside, M.T. (1971) 'Occupational identity, commitment to a trade and attitudes to non-vocational courses amongst a group of craft apprentices', *Vocational Aspect*, 23, 69–72.

Ford, J. (1969) *Social Class and the Comprehensive School*, Routledge and Kegan Paul, London.

Fowler, B., Littlewood, B. and Madigan, R. (1977) 'Immigrant school-leavers and the search for work', *Sociology*, 11, 65–85.

Francome, C. (1983) 'Unwanted pregnancies amongst teenagers', *Journal of Biosocial Science*, 15, 139–143.

Freedman, M. (1969) *The Process of Work Establishment*, Columbia University Press, New York.

Freeman, R.B. (1971) *The Market for College-trained Manpower*, Harvard University Press.

Froyland, E. (1980) *Youth, Education and the World of Work*, Nordic Council of Ministers, Oslo.

Fuller, M. (1980) 'Black girls in a London comprehensive school', in Deem, R. (ed.) *Schooling for Women's Work*, Routledge and Kegan Paul, London.

Garrison, L. (1979) *Black Youth, Rastafarianism and the Identity Crisis in Britain*, Acer Project, London.

Gaskell, G. and Smith, P. (1981) 'Alienated black youth: An investigation of conventional wisdom explanations', *New Community*, 9, 182–193.

Gaskell, J. and Lazerson, M. (1980) *Between School and Work* (mimeo), Faculty of Education, University of British Columbia.

Geer, B. (ed.) (1972) *Learning to Work*, Russell Sage, New York.

Gershuny, J.I. and Pahl, R.E. (1980) 'Britain in the decade of the three economies', *New Society*, 3 January 1980.

Ginzberg, E. (1979) *Good Jobs, Bad Jobs, No Jobs*, Harvard University Press.

Gleeson, D. and Mardle, G. (1980) *Further Education or Training*, Routledge and Kegan Paul, London.

Glyptis, S. (1982) 'Unemployment, sport and recreation: Issues and initiatives in two midland cities'; Paper presented to Leisure Studies Association Conference on Work and Leisure, London.

Gordon, M.S. (1979) *Youth, Education and Unemployment Problems*, Carnegie Council, Berkeley.

Gorz, A. (1972) 'Technical intelligence and the capitalist division of labour', *Telos*, **12**, 27–35.

Gothard, W.P. (1982) *Brightest and Best*, Nafferton Books, Driffield.

Gow, L. and McPherson, A. (eds) (1980) *Tell Them From Me*, Aberdeen University Press.

Graham, K. (1978) Contribution to conference on The Future of Work, Manchester Polytechnic.

Grimond, J. (1979) *Youth Unemployment and the Bridge from School to Work*, Anglo-German Foundation, London.

Gupta, Y.P. (1977) 'The educational and vocational aspirations of Asian immigrant and English school-leavers', *British Journal of Sociology*, **28**, 185–198.

Hale, S. (1971) *The Idle Hill*, Bedford Square Press, London.

Halsey, A.H. Heath, A.F. and Ridge, J.M. (1980) *Origins and Destinations*, Clarendon Press, Oxford.

Hargreaves, D. (1967) *Social Relations in a Secondary School*, Routledge and Kegan Paul, London.

Hargreaves, D. (1982) *The Challenge for the Comprehensive School*, Routledge and Kegan Paul, London.

Hearn, J. (1982), 'Crisis, taboo and careers guidance', *British Journal of Guidance and Counselling*, **9**, 12–23.

Hemborough, A.R. Peevor, R., Speake, B.R. and Whelan, E. (1982) *Work Introduction Courses*, Manpower Services Commission, Research and Development Series 10, London.

Hendry, L.B., Raymond, M. and Stewart, C. (1983) 'Unemployment, school and leisure: An adolescent study', unpublished manuscript, University of Aberdeen.

Henry, S. (1982) 'The working unemployed', *Sociological Review*, **30**, 460–477.

Hesselbart, B. (1977) 'Women doctors win and male nurses lose', *Sociology of Work and Occupations*, **4**, 49–62.

Hill, J. (1978) 'The psychological impact of unemployment', *New Society*, 19 January, 1978.

Hill, J.M.M. and Scharff, D.E. (1976) *Between Two Worlds*, Careers Consultants, London.

Hill, M.J. (1973) *Men Out of Work*, Cambridge University Press.

Hong, L.W. and Duff, R.W. (1977) 'Becoming a taxi-dancer', *Sociology of Work and Occupations*, **4**, 327–342.

Hopper, E. and Osborn, M. (1975) *Adult Students*, Frances Pinter, London.

Hughes, E. (1951) 'Work and the self', in Rohrer, J.H. and Sherif, M. (eds). *Social Psychology at the Crossroads*, Harper and Row, New York.

Hunt, J. and Small, P. (1981) *Employing Young People*, Scottish Council for Research in Education.

Husen, T. (1979) *The School in Question*, Oxford University Press.

Illich, I. (1971) *Deschooling Society*, Calder and Boyars, London.
Illich, I. (1978) *The Right to Useful Unemployment*, Marion Boyars, London.
Income Data Services (1983) *Young Workers' Pay*, Study 291, London.
Institute of Careers Officers (1977) *A Survey of Work Experience in British Secondary Schools*, Stourbridge.
Institute of Careers Officers (1979) *Report of the First Year of the Youth Opportunities Programme*, Stourbridge.
Ipswich National Union of Teachers Working Party (1979) *Job Opportunities in Ipswich for Black School Leavers*, Ipswich National Union of Teachers.
Jackson, M.P. and Hanby, V.J.B. (1982) *British Work Creation Programmes*, Gower, Aldershot.
Jackson, P.R. and Stafford, E.M. (1980) 'Work involvement and employment status as influences on mental health'; Paper presented to British Psychological Society, Canterbury.
Jahoda, G. (1952) 'Job attitudes and job choice among secondary modern school-leavers', *Occupational Psychology*, 26, 125–140 and 206–224.
Jahoda, M. (1979) 'The impact of unemployment in the 1930s and in the 1970s', *Bulletin of the British Psychological Society*, 32, 309–314.
Jahoda, M. (1982) *Employment and Unemployment: A Social-Psychological Analysis*, Cambridge University Press.
Jeanperrin, D. (1979) *Alternating School and Work: Discussion of Current Trends and Prospects* (mimeo), OECD, Paris.
Jenkins, D. (1983) *Community Benefits of Special Programmes in Wales*, Manpower Services Commission, Sheffield.
Jenkins, R. (1982) 'Acceptability, suitability and the search for the habituated worker'; Paper presented to workshop on The Management and Mismanagement of Labour, Loughborough University.
Jewkes, J. and Jewkes, S. (1938) *The Juvenile Labour Market*, Gollancz, London.
Jones, D.C. (1934) *The Social Survey of Merseyside*, Liverpool University Press.
Jones, P., Smith, G. and Pulham, K. (1975) *All Their Future*, Department of Social and Administrative Studies, Oxford University.
Jones, P., Williamson, H., Payne, J. and Smith, G. (1983) *Out of School*, Manpower Services Commission, Special Programmes Occasional Paper 4, Sheffield.
Kaneti-Barry, M., Baldy, R. and van der Eyken, W. (1971) *2100 Sixth Formers*, Hutchinson, London.
Keil, T. (1978) *Becoming a Worker*, Leicester Committee for Education and Industry/Training Services Agency, Leicester.
Keil, E.T., Riddell, D.S. and Green, B.S.R. (1966) 'Youth and work: problems and perspectives', *Sociological Review*, 14, 117–137.
Kelsall, R.K., Poole, A. and Kuhn, A. (1972) *Graduates: the Sociology of an Elite*, Methuen, London.
Kelvin, P. (1981) 'Work as a source of identity: the implications of unemployment', *British Journal of Guidance and Counselling*, 9, 2–11.
King George's Jubilee Trust (1955) *Citizens of Tomorrow*, Odhams, London.

Kitwood, T. (1980) *Disclosures to a Stranger*, Routledge and Kegan Paul, London.

Knasel, E.G., Watts, A.G. and Kidd, J.M. (1982) *The Benefit of Experience*, Manpower Services Commission, Research and Development Series 4, London.

Krause, E. A. (1971) *The Sociology of Occupations*, Little Brown and Company, Boston.

Kreckel, R. (1980), 'Unequal opportunity structure and labour market segmentation', *Sociology*, **14**, 525–550.

Layard, R. (1979) 'Have the Jobcentres increased unemployment?' *Guardian*, 5 November 1979.

Layard, R. (1981) *Unemployment in Britain: Causes and Cures*, Centre for Labour Economics, London School of Economics, Paper 87.

Lazarsfeld, P.F. and Gaudet, H. (1941) 'Who gets a job?' *Sociometry*, **4**, 64–77.

Lee, G.L. and Wrench, K.J. (1981) *In Search of a Skill*, Commission for Racial Equality, London.

Lewis, E.L. (1924) *Children of the Unskilled*, King, London.

Liepmann, K. (1960) *Apprenticeship*, Routledge and Kegan Paul, London.

Logan, R.F.M. and Goldberg, E.M. (1954) 'Rising 18 in a London suburb', *British Journal of Sociology*, **4**, 323–345.

Maddock, I. (1978) in *The Future of Work*, report of a conference held at Manchester Polytechnic.

Maizels, J. (1970) *Adolescent Needs and the Transition from School to Work*, Athlone Press, London.

Makeham, P. (1980) *Youth Unemployment*, Department of Employment Research Paper 11, London.

Manchester City Council Planning Department (1979) *School-leavers and Jobs*, Manchester City Council.

Mann, M. (1973) *Workers on the Move*, Cambridge University Press.

Mann, P.H. (1966) *Young Men and Work*, Department of Sociological Studies, University of Sheffield.

Manpower Services Commission (1977) *Young People and Work*, HMSO, London.

Manpower Services Commission (1979) *Review of the First Year of Special Programmes*, HMSO, London.

Manpower Services Commission (1981a) *A New Training Initiative: a Consultative Document*, HMSO, London.

Manpower Services Commission (1981b) *A New Training Initiative: an Agenda for Action*, HMSO, London.

Manpower Services Commission (1982) *Youth Task Group Report*, HMSO, London.

Manwaring, T. (1982) 'The extended internal labour market'; Paper presented to a workshop on The Management and Mismanagement of Labour, Loughborough University.

Marini, M.M. and Greenberger, E. (1978) 'Sex differences in occupational aspirations and expectations', *Sociology of Work and Occupations*, 5, 147–178.

Marsden, D. (1982) *Workless*, Croom Helm, London.

Merton, R.K., Reader, G.G. and Kendall, P.L. (eds) (1957) *The Student Physician*, Harvard University Press.

Metcalf, D. (1982) *Alternatives to Unemployment*, Policy Studies Institute, London.

Millward, N. (1968) 'Family status and behaviour at work', *Sociological Review*, 16, 149–164.

Ministry of Labour and National Service (1945) *Recruitment and Training of Juveniles for Industry*, HMSO, London.

Moor, C.H. (1976) *From School to Work*, Sage, London.

Morley-Bunker, N. (1982) 'Perceptions of unemployment'; paper presented to the British Psychological Society, Sussex.

Murray, C. (1978) *Youth Unemployment*, National Foundation for Educational Research, Windsor.

Murray, J. and Orwell S. (1972) *School Leavers: Case Studies on London and Sunderland*, Research Institute for Social Policy, London.

National Association of Headteachers (1978) *Memorandum addressed to the House of Commons Expenditure Committee: Social Services and Employment sub-committee enquiry—Employment and Training in the New Unemployment Situation*, National Association of Headteachers, London.

National Youth Employment Council (1974) *Unqualified, Untrained and Unemployed*, HMSO, London.

Newsom Report (1963) *Half Our Future*, Central Advisory Council for Education, HMSO, London.

Norris, G.M. (1978) 'Unemployment, subemployment and personal characteristics', *Sociological Review*, 26, 89–108 and 327–347.

O'Connor, D. (1981) 'Probability of unemployment on leaving work experience schemes', *Government Economic Service Working Paper 53*, Manpower Services Commission, London.

Organisation for Economic Co-operation and Development (1980) *Youth Unemployment: The Causes and Consequences*, OECD, Paris.

Pahl, R.E. (1978) 'Living without a job: How school-leavers see the future', *New Society*, 2 November 1978.

Pahl, R.E. (1982) 'Family, community and unemployment', *New Society*, 21 January 1982.

Pahl, R.E. and Wallace, C. (1980) *17–19 and Unemployed on the Isle of Sheppey*, University of Kent.

Palmer, V.C. (1964) 'Young workers in their first jobs', *Occupational Psychology*, 38, 99–113.

Parkinson, M. (1970) *The Labour Party and the Organisation of Secondary Education*, Routledge and Kegan Paul London.

Parry, S.J. (1980) 'Leisure and unemployment in an industrial society'; Unpublished BEd Dissertation, St Katherine's College, Liverpool.

Pearce, B., Varney, E., Flegg, D. and Waldman, P. (1981) *Trainee-Centred Reviewing*, Manpower Services Commission, Research and Development Series 2, London.
Pedley, R. (1963) *The Comprehensive School*, Penguin, Harmondsworth; revised 1966 and 1969.
Pedley, R. (1977) *Towards the Comprehensive University*, Macmillan, Basingstoke.
Pelican, A., Tucker, S., Rose, C. and Sawdon, A. (1981) *Study of the Transition from School to Working Life: Second Main Report*, Youthaid, London.
Phillips, D. (1973) 'Young and unemployed in a northern city', in Weir, D. (ed.) *Men and Work in Modern Britain*, Fontana, London.
Plummer, J. (1978) *Movement of Jah People*, Press Gang, Birmingham.
Pollock, G.J. and Nicholson, V.M. (1981) *Just the Job*, Hodder and Stoughton, Sevenoaks.
Pryce, K. (1979) *Endless Pressure*, Penguin, Harmondsworth.
Rathkey, P. (1978) Unemployment on Teeside, unpublished manuscript.
Rawstron, E.M. and Coates, B.E. (1966) 'Opportunity and affluence', *Geography*, 51, 1-15.
Rees, T.L. and Atkinson, P. (eds) (1982) *Youth Unemployment and State Intervention*, Routledge and Kegan Paul, London.
Reimer, E. (1971) *School is Dead*, Penguin, Harmondsworth.
Reimer, J.W. (1977) 'Becoming a journeyman electrician', *Sociology of Work and Occupations*, 4, 87-98.
Reubens, B.G. (1977) *Bridges to Work*, Martin Robertson, Oxford.
Rex, J. and Tomlinson, S. (1979) *Colonial Immigrants in a British City*, Routledge and Kegan Paul, London.
Ridley, F.F. (1981) 'View from a disaster area; unemployed youth in Merseyside', *Political Quarterly*, 52, 16-27.
Rist, R.C. (1982) *Earning and Learning*, Sage, London.
Robbins Report (1963) *Higher Education*, Committee on Higher Education, HMSO, London.
Roberts, K. (1967), 'The incidence and effects of spare-time employment amongst school children', *Vocational Aspect*, 11, 129-136.
Roberts, K. (1968a) 'The entry into employment: an approach towards a general theory', *Sociological Review*, 16, 165-184.
Roberts, K. (1968b) 'The organisation of education and the ambitions of school-leavers: a comparative review', *Comparative Education*, 4, 87-96.
Roberts, K. (1971) *From School to Work*, David and Charles, Newton Abbot.
Roberts, K. (1975) 'The developmental theory of occupational choice: a critique and an alternative' in Esland, G., Salaman, G. and Speakman, M. (eds) *People and Work*, Holmes McDougall, Edinburgh.
Roberts, K. (1977) 'The social conditions, consequences and limitations of careers guidance', *British Journal of Guidance and Counselling*, 5, 1-9.
Roberts, K. (1981a) 'The sociology of work entry and occupational choice', in

Watts, A.G., Super, D.E. and Kidd, J.M. (eds) *Career Development in Britain*, Hobsons, Cambridge.

Roberts, K. (1981b), *Unemployment as Experienced by Young People* (mimeo), OECD, Paris.

Roberts, K. (1983) *Youth and Leisure*, Allen and Unwin, London.

Roberts, K., Duggan, J. and Noble, M. (1981) *Unregistered Youth Unemployment and Outreach Careers Work, Part One, Non-registration*, Department of Employment Research Paper 31, London.

Roberts, K., Duggan, J. and Noble, M. (1983) 'Racial disadvantage in youth labour markets', in Barton, L. and Walker, S. (eds.) *Race, Class and Education*, Croom Helm, London.

Roberts, K., Noble, M. and Duggan, J. (1982a) *Unregistered Youth Unemployment and Outreach Careers Work, Part Two, Outreach Careers Work*, Department of Employment Research Paper 32, London.

Roberts, K., Noble, M. and Duggan, J. (1982b) Youth unemployment: An old problem or a new life-style?' *Leisure Studies*, 1, 171–182.

Robinson, E. (1968) *The New Polytechnics*, Penguin, Harmondsworth.

Rosenberg, M. (1957) *Occupations and Values*, Free Press, Clencoe.

Rousselet, J. (1979) *Training and Work: What Youth Perceives and Expects* (mimeo), OECD, Paris.

Rowntree, B.S. and Lasker, B. (1911) *Unemployment: a Special Study*, Macmillan, London.

Ryrie, A.C., Furst, A. and Lauder, M. (1979) *Choices and Chances*, Hodder and Stoughton, London.

Ryrie, A.C. and Weir, A.D. (1978) *Getting a Trade*, Hodder and Stoughton, London.

Sawdon, A. and Taylor, D. (1980) *Youth Unemployment*, Youthaid, London.

Scholzman, K.L. and Verba, S. (1980) *Insult to Injury*, Harvard University Press.

Schools Council Enquiry (1968) *Young School-leavers*, HMSO, London.

Scott, W.H. *et al.* (1956) *Technological Change and Industrial Relations*, Liverpool University Press.

Secretaries of State for Education and Science, for Employment, and for Wales (1979) *Education and Training for 16–18 Year Olds: a Consultative Paper*, HMSO, London.

Shanks, K. (1982) *After Community Industry*, Community Industry, London.

Showler, B. and Sinfield, A. (eds) (1981) *The Workless State*, Martin Robertson, Oxford.

Simpson, I.H. (1979) *From Student to Nurse*, Cambridge University Press.

Sinfield, A. (1981) *What Unemployment Means*, Martin Robertson, Oxford.

Smith, D.J. (1977) *Racial Disadvantage in Britain*, Penguin, Harmondsworth.

Smith, D.V.L. and Sugarman, L. (1981) 'An evaluation of the government's work experience programme for the young unemployed', *British Journal of Guidance and Counselling*, 9, 65–73.

Smith, M.A. and Simpkins, A.F. (1980) *Unemployment and Leisure*, Centre for Leisure Studies and Research, University of Salford.

Smith, S. and Lasko, R. (1978), 'After the work experience programme', *Department of Employment Gazette*, 86, 901–907.

Squires, G.D. (1979) *Education and Jobs*, Transaction Books, New Jersey.

Stafford, E., Jackson, P. and Banks, M. (1980) 'Employment, work involvement and mental health in less qualified young people', *Journal of Occupational Psychology*, 53, 291–304.

Stares, R., Imberg, D. and McRobie, J. (1982) *Ethnic Minorities*, Manpower Services Commission, Research and Development Series 6, London.

Stern, J. (1982) 'Does unemployment really kill?' *New Society*, 10 June 1982.

Stevens, A. (1980) *Clever Children in Comprehensive Schools*, Penguin, Harmondsworth.

Stone, M. (1981) *The Education of the Black Child in Britain*, Fontana, London.

Stonier, T. (1983) *The Wealth of Information*, Methuen, London.

Straus, M.A. and Holmberg, K.H. (1968) 'Part-time employment, social class and achievement in high school', *Sociological and Social Research*, 52, 224–230.

Swann Report (1981) *West Indian Children in our Schools: Committee of Inquiry into the education of children from ethnic minority groups, Interim Report*, HMSO, London.

Swift, B. (1973) 'Job orientations and the transition from school to work: a longitudinal study', *British Journal of Guidance and Counselling*, 1, 62–78.

Sykes, E.G. (1953) 'School and work', *Sociological Review*, 1, 29–47.

Taylor, W. (1963 *The Secondary Modern School*, Faber and Faber, London.

Tenen, C. (1947a) 'The adolescent in the factory', *British Journal of Educational Psychology*, 17, 72–82.

Tenen, C. (1947b) 'Some problems of discipline among adolescents in factories', *Occupational Psychology*, 21, 75–81.

Thomas, R.K. (1979) *Starting Work and After*, Office of Population, Censuses and Surveys, London.

Thomas, R. and Wetherall, D. (1974) *Looking Forward to Work*, HMSO, London.

Toffler, A. (1970), *Future Shock*, Random House, New York.

Tomlinson, J. (1982) 'Unemployment and policy in the 1930 and 1980s', *The Three Banks Review*, 135, 17–33.

Town, S. (1983) 'Recreation and the unemployed: experiments in Bradford', *Leisure Studies Association Newsletter*, 4, 5–10

Turner, R.H. (1960) 'Sponsored and contest mobility in the school system', *American Sociological Review*, 25, 855–867.

Venables, E. (1967) *The Young Worker at College*, Faber and Faber, London.

Veness, T. (1962) *School-leavers*, Methuen, London.

Waddington, P.A.J. (1982) 'Indeterminacy in occupational recruitment: the case of prison assistant governors', *Sociology*, 16, 203–219.

Wallace, C. (1980) 'Adapting to unemployment', *Youth in Society*, 40, 6–8.

Watts, A.G. (1978) 'The implications of school-leaver unemployment for careers education in schools', *Journal of Curriculum Studies*, 10, 233–250.

Watts, A.G. (1980) *Work Experience Programmes—the Views of British Youth*, OECD, Paris.

Watts, A.G. (1981) 'Careers education and the informal economies', *British Journal of Guidance and Counselling*, 9, 22–35.

Watts, A.G., Super, D.E. and Kidd, J.M. (eds) (1981) *Career Development in Britain*, Hobsons, Cambridge.

Watts, C. (1980) *Black Prospects*, South Liverpool Personnel, Liverpool.

Weisman, C.S. *et al.* (1976) 'Sex differences in response to a blocked career pattern among unaccepted medical school applicants', *Sociology of Work and Occupations*, 3, 187–208.

West, M. and Newton, P. (1983) *The Transition from School to Work*, Croom Helm, London.

White, S. (n.d.), Unemployment on Merseyside, unpublished manuscript.

Wilby, P. (1979) 'Streaming and standards', in Pluckrose, H. and Wilby, P. (eds) *The Condition of English Schooling*, Penguin, Harmondsworth.

Wilkins, L.T. (1955) *The Adolescent in Britain*, Central Office of Information, London.

Williams, G. (1957) *Recruitment to Skilled Trades*, Routledge and Kegan Paul, London.

Williams, G. (1963) *Apprenticeship in Europe*, Chapman and Hall, London.

Williams, G. (1969) 'The revolution in industrial training', *Sociological Review Monograph*, 13, 89–103.

Willis, M. (1979) *Youth Unemployment and Leisure Opportunities* (mimeo), Department of Education and Science, London.

Willis, P. (1977) *Learning to Labour*, Saxon House, Farnborough.

Willmott, P. (1966) *Adolescent Boys of East London*, Routledge and Kegan Paul, London.

Wilson, H. and Womersley, L. (1977) *Getting a Job*, Department of the Environment, London.

Wilson, M.D. (1953) 'The vocational preferences of secondary modern school-children', *British Journal of Educational Psychology*, 23, 97–113 and 163–179.

Wood, S. (ed.) (1982) *The Degradation of Work*, Hutchinson, London.

Woods, P. (1976) 'The myth of subject choice', *British Journal of Sociology*, 27, 130–143.

Wray, M.J., Moor, C. and Hill, S. (1980) *Unified Vocational Preparation: an evaluation of the pilot programme*, National Foundation for Educational Research, Windsor.

Yates, J. and Hall, B. (1982), *What Chance Work?* Chesire County Council Careers Service.

Youthaid (1979) *Study of the Transition from School to Working Life*, Youthaid, London.

Youthaid (1981) *Quality or Collapse?* Youthaid, London.

Index

Abrams, M.   28
Absenteeism   16, 51
Adams, D.   51, 66
Additionality rule   92
Adelson, J.   56
Adolescence   6-7, 70
Allen, S.   21, 52, 53, 56
Alternation   101
Anderson, N.   37
Apprenticeship   2, 26-27, 29-34, 47, 83, 92, 104
Ashton, D. N.   22, 26, 36, 40, 48, 50, 51, 56, 84
Aspirations   39-40, 42, 44, 54, 56
Assisted places   13
Atkinson, P.   82, 88

Barrow, R.   108
Baxter, J. L.   43, 67
Bayly, L. P.   85
Becker, H. S.   41
Bedeman, T.   85
Bellaby, P.   15
Beloe Report   14
Benn, C.   14
Berg, I.   23
Bevington, S.   3
Bhroin, N. B.   28
Black economy   71
Black Papers   19
Braverman, H.   105
Brelsford, P.   81, 86
Bresnick, D.   86, 104

Brooks, D.   52
Bunker, N.   74
Burgess, T.   21, 108

Cameron, C.   2
Careers education   21-22, 36-37, 39
Careers Service   33, 37, 65-66, 84
Carmichael, D. M.   20
Carnegie Trust   2, 4
Carper, J. W.   41
Carr Report   33
Carter, M. P.   21, 36, 37, 38
Cashmore, E.   55
Casual employment   70
Central Policy Review Staff   21, 34
Centre for Contemporary Cultural Studies   19
Cherry, N.   73
Child Labour   2, 99
Ching, J. E.   22
Closs, J.   56
Coates, B. E.   29
Colledge, M.   48, 50, 51
Colleges of Education   18, 56
Collins, R.   23
Commission for Racial Equality   53
Community education   18-19
Community Enterprise Programme   81
Community Industry   83-84
Community Programme   81
Comprehensive Schools   4, 14, 106-107

Conant, J. B.　74
Cox, C. B.　19
Credentials　23–24, 99, 107
Crime　72
Crowther Report　14, 25–26, 27, 28, 35
Cunnison, J.　29–36
Cyclical unemployment　59

Daniel, W. W.　65
Davies, B.　100
Davis, D. J.　96–110
Denmark　111
Deschooling　19, 108
Dewberry, C.　74
Dex, S.　52, 58
Donovan, A.　57, 71
Dore, R.　23
Douglas, J. W. B.　14
Douvan, E. A.　56
Driscoll, J.　86
Driver, G.　53
Duggan, J.　44, 67
Duff, R. W.　42
Duffy, J. A.　80, 82, 86
Dungate, M.　81
Dyson, A. E.　19

Eager, W. M.　2, 3, 4
Education　11–24
Eggleston, J.　72
Elder, G. H.　73
Eleven-plus　12–13
Employment and Training Act　33, 90
Ethnic Minorities　52–55, 76, 96–97
Examinations　14–15, 23–24, 107

Factory Acts　2
Ferguson, T.　29, 36
Field, D.　22, 36, 40
Fleming Report　13
Flude, R. A.　41
Ford, J.　16
Fowler, B.　52
France　31, 106

Francis, H.　58
Freedman, M.　43
Freeman, R. B.　23
Froyland, E.　108
Fuller, M.　53
Furst, A.　39
Further education　16–17, 25–27

Garland, V.　48
Garrison, L.　55
Gaskell, G.　75
Gaudet, H.　38
Geer, B.　41
Gender　6, 16, 26, 29, 55–58, 76
Generic skills　105, 110–111
Ginzberg, E.　100
Gleeson, D.　27
Goldberg, E. M.　43
Gordon, M. S.　74
Gorz, A.　105
Gothard, W. P.　22
Grimond, J.　104, 105, 106
Gupta, Y. P.　54

Hale, S.　35
Hall, B.　31–48, 59
Halsey, A. H.　19
Hanby, V. J. B.　66, 86
Hargreaves, D.　39, 99
Harvey, J.　85
Health　70, 71
Heath, A. F.　19
Hearn, J.　70
Hemborough, A. R.　82
Hendry, L. B.　70, 76
Henry, S.　70
Hesselbart, B.　57
Hidden curriculum　22–23, 39–40, 56
Higher education　17–18, 93
Hill, J.　69
Hill, J. M. M.　37
Hill, S.　91
Hong, L. W.　42
Hughes, E.　41
Husen, T.　107

Illich, I.　19, 74, 108

Imberg, D. 55
Ince Report 25, 26, 31, 34, 100, 104
Independent Schools 13
Industrial Training Act 33, 90
Information technology 59-60, 98, 108
Information Technology Centres 87
Institute of Careers Officers 20, 84
Internal labour markets 51

Jackson, M. P. 66, 86
Jackson, P. R. 71
Jahoda, M. 66, 86
Japan 104
Jeanperrin, D. 101
Jenkins, D. 80, 81
Jenkins, R. 52
Jewkes, J. and S. 2
Job-changing 35-37, 40, 43, 64, 67
Job Creation Projects 80-81
Job-finding 37-38, 40, 51-52
Job Release Scheme 89-98, 103
Job satisfaction 38-39
Job splitting 89, 98, 103
Job subsidies 80, 81, 88-89, 110
Jones, D. C. 3
Jones, P. 85-97

Kaneti-Barry, M. 22
Keil, T. 21, 52
Kelsall, R. K. 22, 52
Kelvin, P. 70, 74
Kendall, P. L. 41
Kidd, J. M. 85
King George's Jubilee Trust 36
Knasel, E. G. 85
Krause, E. A. 43

Labour markets 40, 48-49, 95
Labour Party 14, 95, 106
Lasker, B. 46
Lasko, R. 85
Lauder, M. 39
Layard, R. 45, 111
Lazarsfeld, P. F. 38
Lazerson, M. 75

Lee, G. L. 50, 52
Leisure 70, 74, 94, 98, 102-103
Lewis, E. L. 3
Liepmann, K. 30
Littlewood, B. 52
Llewellyn, G. 48
Logan, R. F. M. 43
Long-term unemployment 67-68
Lush, A. 2

McRobie, J. 55
Madigan, R. 52
Maguire, M. J. 26, 48, 51, 56
Maizels, J. 36, 38
Mann, M. 43
Manpower Services Commission 12, 25, 31, 33, 47, 51, 53, 65, 68, 80, 82, 83, 87, 90, 92, 93, 95, 96, 100, 103, 105, 106
Manwaring, T. 51
Mardle, G. 27
Marsden, D. 69
Meara, G. 2
Mental illness 71
Merton, R. K. 41
Metcalf, D. 84
Millward, N. 28
Moor, C. H. 21, 91
Morley-Bunker, N. 70, 74
Murray, J. 29

National Civil Service 86-87
National Youth Employment Council 25, 48
Newsom Report 14
Newton, P. 21
New Training Initiative 26, 31, 34, 90-92, 105
Nicholson, V. M. 21, 65
Noble, M. 44, 67
Norris, G. M. 64

O'Connor, D. 85
Occupational choice 36-37, 39-40, 41-42
Occupational socialization 41-43

Occupational structure   5, 31, 43–44, 59, 110–111
Oddy, M.   57, 71
Orwell, S.   29

Pahl, R. E.   72, 73
Palmer, V. C.   40
Parkinson, M.   14
Parry, S. J.   74
Part-time employment   89, 101
Payne, J.   85
Pearce, B.   85
Pedley, R.   13, 108
Phillips, D.   66, 73
Politics   66, 72, 111
Pollock, G. J.   21, 65
Polytechnics   17–18, 93
Positive action   55
Positive discrimination   18–19, 55
Pratt, J.   21
Pryce, K.   54

Qualifications   49–51

Racial discrimination   52–53
Rastafarians   55
Rathkey, P.   66
Rawstron, E. M.   29
Raymond, M.   70
Reader, G. G.   41
Rees, T. L.   82, 88
Reimer, E.   19, 108
Reimer, J. W.   41
Reubens, B. G.   37
Rex, J.   55
Ridge, J. M.   19
Ridley, F. F.   72
Riots   72
Rist, R. C.   75
Rix, A.   81
Robbins Report   17, 27
Roberts, K.   22, 28, 40, 42, 44, 53, 54, 57, 61, 65, 66, 67, 68, 70, 109, 110
Robinson, E.   17
Rousselet, J.   74
Rowntree, B. S.   46

Ryrie, A. C.   30, 32, 34, 37, 39

Sawdon, A.   51, 59, 66
Scharff, D. E.   37
Scholzman, K. L.   63
School-leaving age   13, 15, 27
Scott, W. H.   42
Secretan, H. A.   2–3, 4
Sex discrimimation   56
Shanks, K.   84
Shift-work   48
Simon, B.   14
Simpson, I. H.   41
Sinfield, A.   69
Singh, K.   52
Skillcentres   32
Smith, C. R.   21, 52, 53, 56
Smith, D. J.   53
Smith, D. V. L.   85
Smith, G.   81
Smith, S.   85
Socialism   9–10, 113–114
Social Survey of Merseyside   3
Soviet Union   9–10, 106
Spare-time jobs   8
Special measures   67, 78–97
Special Temporary Employment Programme   81
Squires, G. D.   23
Stafford, E.   71
Stares, R.   55
Stern, J.   70
Stevens, A.   16
Stewart, C.   70
Stilgoe, E.   65
Stone, M.   54
Stonier, T.   6
Structural unemployment   59–60
Sub-employment   64–67
Sugarman, L.   85
Supplementary Benefit   61, 83, 93
Swann Report   52
Sweden   107
Sykes, E. G.   35

Taylor, D.   59

Taylor, W.   14
Technical education   20, 21, 92, 106–107
Technological change   59–60, 98, 102, 104
Tenen, C.   36
Thomas, R. K.   21
Tomlinson, J.   46
Tomlinson, S.   55
Town, S.   63, 70
Trainee-centred reviewing   85
Training   6, 25–34, 47, 83, 90–92, 93–94, 99–100, 103–106
Training for Skills Programme   83, 93
Truancy   16, 51

Unemployment rates   46–47, 51, 53, 61–62, 65, 80, 105
Unified Vocational Preparation   91
United States of America   74–75, 107, 109
Universities   17, 93
Unregistered unemployment   61

Verba, S.   63
Vocational training, *see* Training
Vouchers   108

Waddington, P. A. J.   42
Wage-levels   27, 88–89, 91, 96
Ward, V.   48
Watts, A. G.   70, 79, 85

Watts, C.   52
Weir, A. D.   30, 32, 34, 37
Weisman, C. S.   56
West, M.   21
West Germany   31, 103–105
Wetherall, D.   21
White, S.   59
Wilby, P.   107
Wilkins, L. T.   43, 56
Williams, G.   30, 33
Williamson, H.   85
Willis, M.   74
Willis, P.   22, 40, 42
Wilson, H.   51
Womersley, L.   51
Wood, S.   105
Woods, P.   39
Work experience   20, 108
Work Experience on Employers Premises   81–82, 86, 87
Work Experience Programme   81
Work Preparation   82
Wray, M. J.   91
Wrench, K. J.   50, 52

Yates, J.   31, 48–59
Young Workers Scheme   88–89, 90
Youthaid   21, 37, 38, 48, 49, 65, 66
Youth Opportunities Programme   27, 68, 81–83, 84–88, 100
Youth Training Scheme   90–92, 103, 105